D1126202

NOSTRADAMUS
The Complete Prophecies
For the Future

Les Propheties (The Prophecies)
Was published in 1555 by
Michel de Nostredame (aka Nostradamus)

It was translated from French to English in 1672 by
Theophilus Garencières

This illustrated edition was produced in 2023

Design and illustrations by
Ari Cloris

Ari Cloris

TABLE OF CONTENTS

NOSTRADAMUS

Michel de Nostredame, usually Latinised as Nostradamus is one of the most famous figures in history. He was a French astrologer and physician who is widely known for his prophetic prophecies. He was born in France in 1503 and died in 1566. His predictions have been studied for centuries and have been featured in popular culture. He is widely credited with predicting wars and natural disasters, as well as the rise and fall of power and governments.

Nostradamus claimed to be able to predict the future using astrological methods. He wrote many books that contained his prophetic verses and interpretations of the stars and planets. His books have sold millions of copies and have been translated into many languages. Nostradamus' prophecies are still studied today, with many believers believing that his predictions are coming true.

Nostradamus made many predictions that were incredibly accurate. He predicted the French Revolution, the rise of Napoleon, and the Great fire of London. He also claimed to have predicted the assassination of President John F. Kennedy and the destruction of the Twin towers. His predictions are still studied by historians and believers today, and some believe that his predictions are still coming true.

Source: Wikipedia

The portrait of Michel de Nostredame, A French Renaissance Medicine & Astrologer, painted by his son César de Nostredame.

Nostradamus' importance in history is largely due to his prophecies. They have helped shape the way we view the world and our place in it. His predictions have influenced many events in history, and his legacy will likely continue to be studied for centuries to come.

No matter what one believes about Nostradamus, his legacy and importance in history cannot be denied. He was one of the most famous figures of his time and his prophecies are still studied today. He has had a lasting impact on the way we view the world, and his predictions have shaped events for centuries. Nostradamus' importance in history is undeniable, and his legacy will live on for years to come.

THE PROPHECIES

Nostradamus's book, The Prophecies, is a collection of 942 predictive quatrains written in the 16th century. The quatrains are divided into ten groups of one hundred, often referred to as a "century." However, it is important not to jump to the conclusion that the prophecies referred to cover 100 years. Centuries and years are not directly related in this context, and the arrangement of the 942 prophecies is done simply to facilitate organization. Additionally, Century 7 has only about half the number of quatrains, and the reason why Nostradamus chose to do this remains unknown.

The Prophecies are written in a cryptic style, with the use of symbolism and anagrams. This makes them difficult to interpret, as the reader must decipher the imagery and symbols used. Many of Nostradamus's quatrains are seen as vague and open to interpretation, which has led some to believe that the prophecies are merely a tool for predicting the future, rather than predicting specific events.

The quatrains are often seen as being divided into two parts – the first part being a prediction of the future, while the second part is a description of the events that will lead to the prediction. For example, a quatrain may predict the fall of a certain ruler, and the second part of the quatrain will describe the events that will lead to this fall. This type of structure has led some to believe that Nostradamus's prophecies contain a hidden meaning.

Nostradamus's book is among the most famous works of prophetic literature, and has inspired countless works of fiction, as well as countless interpretations. While many people take Nostradamus's prophecies seriously, it is important to note that the quatrains are still open to interpretation and that it is impossible to know for certain what the future holds. Thus, Nostradamus's book of The Prophecies should be viewed as an entertaining and thought-provoking work of literature, not as a reliable source of predictions.

LES
PROPHETIES
DE M. MICHEL
NOSTRADAMVS.

Dont il y en a trois cens qui n'ont encores iamais efté imprimées.

Adiouftées de nouueau par lediét Autheur.

A LYON,
PAR BENOIST RIGAVD.
1568.
Auec permiffion.

Title page of Les Prophéties of Nostradamus (Lyon, 1568).

CENTURY I

1

Sitting by night in my secret study
Alone, resting upon the brazen stool,
A slight flame breaking forth out of that solitude,
Makes me utter what is not in vain to believe.

2

With Rod in hand, set in the middle of the branches,
With water I wet the limb and the foot,
In fear I writ, quaking in my sleeves,
Divine splendor, the divine sitteth by.

3

When the litter shall be overthrown by a gust of wind,
And faces shall be covered with cloaks,
The commonwealth shall be troubled with a new kind of men,
Then white and red shall judge amiss.

4

In the World shall be one monarch,
Who shall be not long alive, nor in peace,
Then shall be lost the fishing boat,
And be governed with worse detriment.

5

They shall be driven away without great fighting,
Those of the country shall be more grieved,
Town and city shall have a greater debate,
Carcassonne and Narbonne will have their hearts tried.

6

The eye of Ravenna shall be forsaken,
When the wings shall rise at his feet,
The two of Brescia shall have constituted,
Turin and Vercelli, which the Gauls will trample.

7

One coming too late, the execution shall be done,
The wind being contrary, and letters intercepted by the way,
The conspirators fourteen of asect,
By the red-haired man the undertaking shall be made.

8

How often taken o solar city,
Shalt thou be? changing the barbarian and vain laws,
Thy evil growth nigh, thou shalt be more tributary,
The great Adria shall recover thy veins.

9

From the East shall come the African heart,
To vex Adria, and the heirs of Romulus,
Accompanied with the Libian fleet
Melites shall tremble, and the neighbouring islands be empty.

10

Sergeants sent into an iron cage,
Where the seven children of the king are,
The old men and fathers shall come out of hell,
And before they die shall see the death and cries of their fruit.

11

The motion of the senses, heart, feet and hands,
Shall agree, Naples, Lyon, Sicily,
Swords, fires, waters, then to the noble Romans,
Killed or dead because of a weak brain.

12

Within a little while a false frail brute shall go,
From low to high, being quickly raised,
By reason that he shall have the government of Verona,
Shall be unfaithful and slippery.

13

The banished, by choler, and intestine hatred
Shall make against the king a great conspiracy,
They shall put secret enemies in the mine,
And the old his own against them sedition.

14

From slavish people, songs, tunes and requests,
Being kept prisoners by princes and lords,
For the future by headless idiots,
Shall be admitted by divine prayers.

15

Mars threatneth us of a warlike force,
Seventy times he shall cause blood to be shed,
The flourishing and ruine of the clergy,
And by those that will hear nothing from them.

16

The Sith to the fish-pond, joyned to sagittarius,
In the highest auge of the exaltation,
Plague, famine, death by a military hand,
The age groweth near to its renovation.

17

During fourty years the rainbow shall not appear,
During fourty years it shall be seen every day.
The parched earth shall wax dryer and dryer,
And great floods shall be when it shall appear.

18

Through the discord and negligence of the French,
A passage shall be opened to Mohammedans,
The land and sea of Sienna shall be bloody,
And the port of Marseilles covered with ships and sails.

19

When serpents shall come to encompass the are,
The Trojan blood shall be vexed by Spain,
By them, a great number shall perish,
Chief runneth away, and is hid in the rushes of the marshes.

20

The cities of Tours, Orleans, Blois, Angers, Reims and Nantes
Cities vexed by a sudden change,
By strange languages tents shall be set up,
rivers, darts at Rennes, shaking of land and sea.

21

A deep white clay feedeth a rock,
Which clay shall break out of the deep like milk,
In vain people shall be troubled not daring to touch it,
Being ignorant that in the bottom there is a milky clay.

22

That which shall live, and shall have no sence,
The lion shall destroy the art of it,
Autun, Chalons, Langres, and both Sens,
The war and the Ice shall do great harm.

23

In the third month at the rising of the sun,
The boar and leopard in marth camp to fight;
The leopard weary, lift his eyes to heaven,
And seeth an eagle playing about the sun.

24

In the new city for to condemn a prisoner,
The bird of pray shall offer himself to heaven,
After the victory, the prisoners shall be forgiven,
After Cremona and Mantua have suffered many troubles.

25

Lost, found again, hidden so great a while,
A pastor will be celebrated almost as a god-like figure.
But before the moon endeth her great age,
By other winds he shall be dishonoured.

26

The great man will be struck down in the day by a thunderbolt.
An evil foretold by a common porter;
According to this foretelling another falleth in the night,
A fight at Reims, and the plague at London and Tuscany.

27
Under the oak Guyen strucken from heaven,
Not far from it is the treasure hidden,
Which hath been many ages a gathering;
Being found he shall die, the eye put out by a spring.

28
The tower of Tobruk shall be in fear of a barbarian fleet,
For a while, and long after afraid of Spanish shipping,
Flocks, peoples, goods both shall receive great damage,
Taurus and libra, o what a deadly feud.

29
When the fish that is both terrestrial and aquatic,
By a strong wave shall be cast upon the sand,
With his strange fearful sweet horrid form,
Soon after the enemies will come near to the walls by sea.

30
The outlandish ship by a sea storm,
Shall come near the unknown haven,
Notwitstanding the signs given to it with bows,
It shall die, be plundered, a good advice come too late.

31
So many years the wars shall last in France,
Beyond the course of the Castulon Mmonarque,
An uncertain victory three great ones shall crown,
The eagle, the cock, the moon, the lion having the sun in its mark.

32
The great empire shall soon be translated,
Into a little place which shall soon grow afterwards.
An inferiour place of a small country,
In the middle of which he shall come to lay down his scepter.

33
A great bridge near a spacious plain,
The great lion by Cæsarean forces,
Shall cause to be pulled down, without the rigorous city,
For fear of which, the gates shall be shut to him.

34
The bird of prey flying to the window,
Before battle, shall appear to the French;
One shall take a good omen of it, the other a bad one,
The weaker part shall hold it for a good sign.

35
The young lion shall overcome the old one,
In Martial field by a single duel,
In a golden cage he shall put out his eye,
Two wounds from one, then he shall die a cruel death.

36
The monarque shall too late repent,
That he hath not put to death his adversary;
But he shall give his consent to a greater thing than that,
Which is to put to death all his adversaries kindred.

37
A little before the sun setteth,
A battle shall be given, a great people shall be doubtful,
Of being foiled, the sea-port maketh no answer,
A bridge and sepulchre shall be in two strange places.

38
The sun and the eagle shall appear to the victorious,
A vain answer shall be made good to the vanquished,
By no means arms shall not be stopped,
Vengeance maketh peace, by death he then accomplisheth it.

39

By night in the bed the chief one shall be strangled.
For having too much suborned fair elect,
The empire is enslaved and three men substituted.
He shall put him to death, reading neither card nor packet.

40

The false troup dissembling their folly,
Will cause Byzantium to change its laws
One shall come out of Egypt who will have untied
The edict, changing the coin and allay.

41

A siege laid to a city, and assaulted by night,
Few escaped, a fight not far from the sea,
A woman swoundeth for joy to see her son returned;
A poison hidden in the fold of letters.

42

The tenth of the Calends of April, gothik account,
Raised up again by malitious persons,
The fire put out, a diabolical assembly,
Shall seek for the bones of Damant and Psellin.

43

Before the change of the empire cometh,
There shall happen a strange accident,
A field shall be changed, and a pillar of prophyry,
Shall be transported upon the chalky rock.

44

Within a little while sacrifices shall come again,
Opposers shall be put to martyrdom;
There shall be no more monks, abbots, nor novices,
Honey shall be much dearer then wax.

45

Follower of sects, great troubles to the messenger,
A beast upon the theatre prepareth the scenical play,
The inventor of that wicked fact shall be famous,
By sects the world shall be confounded and schismatik.

46

Near Auch, Lectoure and Mirande,
A great fire from heaven shall fall three nights together,
A thing shall happen stupendious and wonderful,
A little while after, the earth shall quake.

47

The Ssrmons of the Leman lake shall be troublesome,
Some days shall be reduced into weeks,
Then into months, then into year, then they shall fail,
The magistrates shall condemn their vain laws.

48

Twenty years of the reign of the moon being past,
Seven thousands years another shall hold his monarchy,
When the sun shall reassume his days past,
Then is fulfilled, and endeth my prophecy.

49

A great while before these doings,
Those of the East by the virtue of the moon,
In the year 1700. shall carry away great droves,
And shall subdue almost the whole Northern corner.

50

From the aquatic triplicity shall be born,
One that shall make Thursday his holiday,
His fame, praise, reign, and power shall grow,
By land andsea, and a tempest to the East.

51

Heads of Aries, Jupiter and Saturn,
O eternal god, what changes shall there be!
After a long age his wicked time cometh again,
What turmoil in France and Italy.

52

The two malignants of scorpion being joyned,
The grand seignor murdered in his hall,
Plague to the church by a king newly joyned to it,
The lower parts of Europe and in the North.

53

Alas, how a great people shall be tormented,
And the holy law in an utter ruine;
By other laws, all christianity troubled,
When new mines of gold and silver shall be found.

54

Two revolts shall be made by the wicked scythe bearer,
Which shall make a change of the reign and the age,
The moveable sign doth offer it self for it,
To the two equals in inclination.

55

In the climate opposite to the Babylonian,
There shall be a great effusion of blood.
Insomuch that the land, and sea, air and heaven shall seem unjust
Sects, famine, reigns, plague, confusion.

56

You shall see soon or late great alterations
Extreme horrours and revenges,
The moon leaden by her angel,
The heaven draweth near its inclinations.

57

By great discord, the trumpet shall sound,
Agreement broken, lifting the head to heaven,
A bloody mouth shall swim in blood,
The face turned to the sun anointed with milk and honey.

58

Slit in the belly, shall be born with two heads,
And four arms, it shall live some years,
The day that Aquilare shall celebrate his festivals,
Fossan, Turin, chief Ferrara shall run away.

59

They banished that were carried into the islands,
At the change of a more cruel monarque,
Shall be murdered, and put in the sparks of fire,
Because they had not been sparing of their tongues.

60

An emperor shall be born near Italy,
Who shall cost dear to the empire,
They shall say, what people he keepeth company!
He shall be found less a prince, than a butcher.

61

The miserable and unhappy commonwealth,
Shall be wafted by the new magistrate;
Their great gathering from exiled persons,
Shall cause Swedeland to break her contract.

62

Alas what a great loss shall learning suffer,
Before the circle of the moon be accomplished,
Fire, great flood, and more by ignorant scepters,
Then can be made good again in a long age.

63
The scourges being past, the world shall be diminished,
Peace for a great while, lands inhabited,
Every one safe shall go by heaven, land and sea,
And then the wars shall begin a fresh.

64
They shall think to have seen the sun in the night,
When the hog half a man shall be seen,
Noise, singing, battles in heaven shall be seen to fight,
And brute beasts shall be heard to speak.

65
A child without hands, so great lightning never seen,
The royal child wounded at Tennis,
Bruised at the well, lightnings, going to grind,
Three shall be strucken by the middle.

66
He that then shall carry the news,
A little while after shall draw his breath,
Viviers, Tournon, Montferrant, and Pradelles,
Hail and storm shall make them sigh.

67
What a great famine do I see drawing near,
To turn one way, then another, and then become universal,
So great and long, that they shall come to pluck
The root from the wood, and the child from the breast.

68
O to what a horrid and unhappy torment
Shall be put three Innocents!
Poison shall be suspected, evil keepers shall betray them,
They shall be put to horrour by drunken executioners.

69

The great mount in compass seven stades,
After peace, war, famine, and flooding,
Shall tumble a great way, sinking great countries,
Yea ancient buildings, and great foundation.

70

The rain, famine, war, in Persia being not ceased,
Too great credulity shall betray the monarque;
Being ended there it shall begin in France,
A secret omen to one that he shall die.

71

The sea-tower three times taken and retaken,
By Spaniards, Barbarians, and Ligurians,
Marseilles and Aix, Arles by those of Pisa,
Wast, fire, iron, plunder, Avignon of Thurins.

72

Marseille shall wholly change her Inhabitants
These shall run and be pursued as far as Lyon,
Narbonne, Toulouse angered by Bordeaux;
There shall be killed and taken prisoner almost a million.

73

France by a neglect shall be assaulted on five sides,
Tunis, Algiers stirred up by the Persians.
Lyon, Seville and Barcelona having failed,
And not be pursued by the Venetians.

74

After a stay, they shall sail towards an empire,
The great succours shall come towards Antioch,
The black hair curled, shall aim much to the empire,
The brazen beard shall be roasted on a spit.

75

The tyrant of Sienna shall occupy Savona;
The fort being won, shall hold a fleet,
The two armies shall go in the mark of Ancona,
By fear the chief shall be examined.

76

By a wild name one shall be called
So that the three sisters shall have the name of Fato,
Afterwards a great people by tongue and deeds, shall say,
He shall have fame and renown more than any other.

77

Between two seas shall a promontory be raised,
By him, who shall die by the biting of a horse,
The proud Neptune shall fold the black sail.
Through Calpre, and a fleet shall be near Rocheval.

78

An old head shall beget an idiot,
Who shall degenerate in learning and in arms,
The head of France shall be feared by his sister,
The fields shall be divided and granted to the troopers.

79

Bazas, Lectoure, Condom, Auch and agen
Being moved by laws, quarrels and monopoly,
For they shall put to ruine Bordeaux, Tholose, Bayonne,
Going about to renew their massacre.

80

From the sixth bright celestial splendour,
Shall come very great lightning in Burgundy,
After that shall be born a monster of a most hideous beast,
In March, April, May, June shall be great quarelling and muttering.

81

Nine shall be set aside from the human flock,
Being divided in judgement and counsel
Their fortune shall be to be divided,
Kappa, theta, lambda, dead, banished, scattered.

82

When the wooden columns shall be much shaken,
In the south wind, covered with blood.
Then shall go out a great assembly,
And Vienne, and the land of Austria shall tremble.

83

The stranger agent shall divide booties,
Saturn in Mars shall have his aspect furious,
Horrid, and strange to the Tuscans and Latines,
Greeks who will wish to strike.

84

The moon shall be darkned in the deepest darkness,
Her bother shall pass being of a ferrugineous colour,
The great one long hidden under darkness,
Shall make his iron lukewarm in the bloody rain.

85

A king shall be troubled by the answer of a lady,
Embassadors shall despise their lives,
The great one being double in mind shall counterfeit his bothers,
They shall die by two, anger, hatred, and envy.

86

When the great queen shall see her self vanquished,
She shall do a deed of a masculine courage,
Upon a horse, she shall pass over the river naked,
Followed by iron, she shall do wrong to her faith.

87

Ennosigee, fire of the center of the earth,
Shall make quake about the new city,
Two great rocks shall a great while war one against the other,
After that, Arethusa shall colour red a new river.

88

The divine sickness shall surprise a great prince,
A little while after he hath married a woman,
His support and credit shall at once become slender,
Council shall die for the shaven head.

89

Those of Lerida will be in the Moselle,
Kill all those from the Loire and Seine.
The seaside track will come near the high valley,
When the Spanish open every route.

90

Bourdeaux, Poitiers, at the sound of the bell,
With a great navy shall go as far as Langon,
A great rage will surge up against the French,
When an hideous monster shall be born near Orgon.

91

The gods shall make it appear to man-kind,
That they are the authors of a great war;
For the heaven that was serene, shall shew sword and lance,
Signifying, that on the left hand the affliction shall be greater.

92

Under one shall be peace, and every where clemency,
But not a long while, then shall be plundering and rebellion,
By a denyal shall town, land and sea be assaulted,
There shall be dead and taken prisoners the third part of a million.

93

The Italian land of the mountains shall tremble,
The lion and the cock shall not agree very well together,
Shall for fear help one another,
Freedom alone moderates the French.

94

In the port Selyn the tyrant shall be put to death
And yet the liberty shall not be recovered,
The new Mars by vengeance and remorse,
Lady by excess of fear honoured.

95

Before the monastery shall one twin be found,
From heroic blood, of a monk and ancient,
His fame by sect, tongue, and power shall be sounded,
Is such that they will say the living twin is deservedly chosen.

96

He that shall have charge to destroy,
Churches and sects, changed by fancy;
Shall do more harm to the rocks, than to the living,
By a smooth tongue filling up the ears.

97

What neither iron nor fire could compass,
Shall be done by a smooth tongue in the councel,
In sleep a dream shall make the king to think,
The more the enemy in fire and military blood.

98

The captain that shall lead an infinite deal of people
Far from their country, to one of strange manners and language,
Five thousand will die in Crete and Thessaly, ,
The head running away, shall be safe in a barn by the sea.

99

The great monarch shall keep company,
With two kings united in friendship;
O what fights shall be made by their followers!
Children, o what pity shall be about Narbon.

100

A great while shall be seen in the air a gray bird,
Near Dola and the Tuscan land,
Holding in his bill a green bough;
Then shall a great one die, and the war have and end.

CENTURY II

1

Towards Gascony by English assaults,
By the same shall be made great incursions,
Rains, frosts, shall marre the ground.
Port Selyn shall make strong Invasions.

2

The glue-head shall do the white head
As much harm, as France hath done it good,
Dead at the sail-yard the great one hung on the branch,
When a king taken by his own, shall say, how much?

3

By the heat of the sun upon the sea
Of Negrepont, the fishes shall be half broiled,
The inhabitants shall come to cut them up,
When Rhodes and Genoa shall want Biscuit.

4

From Monaco as far as Sicily,
All the sea coast shall be left desolate,
There shall not be suburbs, cities, nor towns,
Which shall not be pillaged and plundred by Barbarians.

5

When in a fish, iron and a letter shall be shut up,
He shall go out that afterwards shall make war,
He shall have his fleet by sea well provided,
Appearing by the Roman land.

6

Near the gates and within two cities
Shall be two scourges, I never saw the like,
Famine, within plague, people thrust out by the sword,
Shall cry for help to the great god immortal.

7

Among many that shall be transported into the islands,
One shall be born with two teeth in his mouth,
They shall die of hunger, the trees shall be eaten,
They shall have a new king, who shall make new laws for them.

8

Churches consecrated, and the ancient Roman way,
Shall reject the tottering foundations,
Sticking to their first humane laws,
Expelling, but not altogether the worshipping of saints.

9

Nine years shall the lean one keep the kingdom in peace,
Then he will fall into such a bloody thirst,
That a great people shall die without faith or law,
He shall be killed by one milder than himself.

10

Before it be long, all shall be set in order,
We look for a sinister age,
The state of the wisards and of the alone shall be changed,
They shall find few that will keep their ranks.

11

The eldest son of the elder shall prosper,
Being raised to the degree of the great ones,
Every one shall fear his high glory,
But his children shall be cast out.

12
Eyes shut, shall be open by an antick fancy,
The cloths of the alone shall be brought to nothing.
The great monarch shall punish their frenzy,
For having ravished the treasure of the temple before.

13
The body without the soul shall be no more admitted in sacrifice,
The day of the death shall be put for the birthday,
The divine spirit shall make the soul happy,
By seeing the word in its eternity.

14
At Tours, Gien, Gergeau, shall be piercing eyes,
Discovering from afar her serene highness
She and her attendans shall enter into the port,
By a fight shall be thrust out the sovereign power.

15
A little before a monarch be killed
Castor, and pollux shall appear, and a comet in the ship;
The publick brass, by land and sea shall be emptyed,
Pisa, Asti, Ferrara, Turin land under interdict.

16
Naples, Palermo, Sicily, Syracuse,
New tyrants, lightnings, celestial fires,
Force from London, Ghent, Brussels and Susa,
Great slaughter, triumph leads to festivities.

17
The camp of the temple of the vestal virgin,
Not far from Ethene and the Pyrenean mountains,
The great conduit is driven in the bag,
Rivers overflown in the North, and the vines spoiled.

18
A new rain, sudden, impetuous,
Shall suddenly hinder two armies,
Stone, heaven, fire, shall make the sea stony,
The death of seven shall be sudden upon land and sea.

19
New comers shall build a place without fence,
And shall occupy a place that was not then habitable,
They shall at their pleasure take fields, houses and towns.
There shall be famine, plague, war, and a long arable field.

20
Brothers and sisters shall be made slaves in divers places,
And shall pass before the monarch,
Who shall look upon them with attentive eyes,
They shall go in heaviness, witness their chin, forehead and nose.

21
The embassador that was sent in Biremes,
In the midleway shall be repulsed by unknown men,
From the Salt to his succours shall come four triremes,
Ropes and chains shall be carried to Negrepont.

22
The camp Ascop shall go from Europe,
And shall come near the drowned island;
From Arton shall go an army by sea and land,
By the navel of the world a greater vice shall be substituted.

23
Palais birds, driven away by a bird,
Soon after that, the prince is come to his own,
Although the enemy be driven beyond the river,
He shall be seased upon without, by the trick of the bird.

24

Beasts ferocious from hunger will swim across rivers:
The greater part of the region will be against the Hister,
The great one will cause it to be dragged in an iron cage,
When the German child will observe nothing.

25

The garrison of strangers shall betray the fort,
Under the hope and shadow of a higher match,
The garrison shall be deceived, and the fort taken in the crowd,
Loire, Saone, Rhone, Gar, mortal outrage.

26

Because of the favour the city shall shew,
To the great one, who soon after shall loose the battle,
The Thesin shall pour blood into the Po,
Of blood, fire, dead, drowned, by edgeling.

27

The divine word shall be struck by heaven,
So that he shall proceed no further,
The secret of the close keeper, shall be so closed up,
That people shall tread upon, and before it.

28

The last, but one of the surname of the prophet,
Shall take Diana for his day and his rest,
He shall wander far by reason of his frentic head,
Delivering a great people from impositions.

29

The Oriental shall come out of his seat,
Shall pass over the Apennine mountains, and see France,
Shall go over the air, the waters and snow,
And shall strike every one with his rod.

30

One that shall cause the infernal gods of Hannibal
To live again, the terror of mankind,
There was never more horror, not to say ill dayes,
Did happen, or shall, to the Romans by Babel.

31

In campania the Cassilin shall so behave himself,
That one will see only fields covered by waters,
Before, and after it, shall not rain for a good while,
Except the trees, no green shall be seen.

32

Milk, blood, frogs shall reign in Dalmatia,
A battle fought, the plague near Balene,
A great cry shall be through all Slavonia,
Then shall be born a monster, near and within Ravenna.

33

In the torrent which cometh down from Verona,
About the place where it falleth into the Po,
A great shipwrack, and no less in Garonna,
When those of Genoa shall go into their country.

34

The mad anger of the furious fight,
Shall cause by bothers the iron to glister at the table,
To part them one wounded, curious,
The fierce duel shall do harm after in France.

35

The fire shall take by night in two houses,
Many shall be stifled and burnt in it;
Near two rivers it shall for certain happen,
Sun, Sagittarius and capricorn all will be reduced.

36

The letters of the great prophet shall be intercepted,
They shall fall into the hands of the tyrant,
His undertakings shall be to deceive his king,
But his extortions shall trouble him soon.

37

Of that great number which shall be sent,
To succour the besieged in the fort,
Plague and famine shall devour them all,
Except seventy that shall be beaten.

38

There shall be a great number of condemned men,
When the monarchs shall be reconciled,
But one of them shall come to such misfortune,
That their reconciliation shall not last long.

39

One year before the Italian fight,
Germans, French, Spaniards for the fort,
The Schoolhouse of the commonwealth shall fall,
Where, except few, they shall be suffocated, and dead.

40

A little while after, without any great distance of time,
By sea and land shall a great tumult be made,
The sea fight shall be much greater,
Fire and beasts which shall make greater insult.

41

The great star shall burn for the space of seven days,
A cloud shall make two suns appear,
The big mastif shall houl all night,
When the great pope shall change his country.

42

A cock, dogs, and cats shall be fed with blood,
And with the wound of the tyrant found dead,
In the bed of another, with legs and arms broken,
Who could not die before by a cruel death.

43

During the hairy apparent star,
The three great princes shall be made enemies,
Struck from heaven, peace, quakingearth,
Po, Tiber overflowing, serpent placed upon the shore.

44

The eagle flying among the tents,
By other birds shall be driven away,
When noise of cymbals, trumpets, and bells,
Shall render the sense to the lady that was without it.

45

The heaven bemoaneth too much the androgyn born,
Near heaven humane blood shall be spilt,
By death too late a great people shall be refreshed,
Late and soon cometh the succours expected.

46

After a great humane change, another greater is nigh at hand,
The great motor reneweth the ages,
Rain, blood, milk, famine, sword, plague,
In the heaven shall be seen a running fire with long sparks.

47

The great and old enemy grieveth, dieth by poison,
An infinite number of sovereign's conquered,
It shall rain stones, they shall hide under rocks,
In vain shall death alledge articles.

48

The great army that shall pass over the mountains,
Saturn, aries, Mars, turning to the fishes,
Poisons hidden in sheeps heads,
Their war-chief hung with cord.

49

The advisers of the first monopoly,
The conquerers seduced for Malta,
Rhodes, Byzantium for them exposing their pole,
The ground shall fail the followers of runaways.

50

When those of Hainaut, of Ghent and of Brussels
Shall see the siege laid before Langres,
Behind their sides shall be cruel wars,
The old wound shall be worse then enemies.

51

The blood of the just shall be wanting in London,
Burnt by fire of three and twenty, the six,
The antient dame shall fall from her high place,
Of the same sect many shall be killed.

52

During many nights the earth shall quake,
About the spring two great earthquakes shall follow one another,
Corinth, Ephesus shall swim in the two seas,
War shall be moved by two great wrestlers.

53

The great plague of the maritime city,
Shall not cease till the death be revenged
Of the just blood by price condemned without crime,
Of the great dame not fainedly abused.

54

Because of people strange, and distant from the Romans
Their great city much troubled after water:
Daughter handless, domain too different,
Chief taken, lock not having been picked.

55

In the conflict the great one who was worth little
At his end will perform a marvelous deed:
While 'Adria' will see what he was lacking,
During the banquet the proud one stabbed.

56

He whom neither plague, nor sword could destroy,
Shall die in the rain being stricken with thunder,
The abbot shall die when he shall see ruined,
Those in the shipwreck, striving to catch hold of the rock.

57
Before the battle the great one shall fall,
The great one to death too sudden and bewailed;
One shall be born half perfect, the most part shall swim,
Near the river the earth shall be dyed with blood.

58
Without foot or hand, sharp and strong tooth,
By a Globe, in the middle of the port, and the first born,
Near the gate shall be transported by a traitor,
Seline shineth, the little great one carried away.

59
The French fleet by the help of the great guard,
Of great Neptune and his tridentary soldiers
Shall gnaw Provence by keeping great company,
Besides, Mars shall plague Narbon by javelins and darts.

60
The punic faith broken in the East,
Ganges, Jordan, and Rhone, Loire, and Tagus will change,
When the mules hunger shall be satisfied,
The fleet scattered, blood and bodies shall swim.

61
Agen, Tonneins, Gironde and La Rochelle,
O Trojan blood death is at the harbour of the arrow,
Beyond the river the ladder shall be raised against the fort,
Points, fire, great murder upon the breach.

62
Mabus shall come, and soon after shall die,
Of people and beasts shall be an horrible destruction,
Then on a sudden the vengeance shall be seen,
Blood, hand, thirst, famine, when the comet shall run.

63
The French shall a little subdue Ausonne,
Po, Marne and Seine Parma will make drunk,
Which shall raise a great wall against them,
From the less to the wall the great one shall loose his life.

64
Those of Geneva shall be dried up with hunger and thirst,
A near hope shall come when they shall be fainting,
The Gebenna law shall be upon a quaking point,
The navy shall not be capable to come into the port.

65
The park enclineth to great calamity,
Which shall be through Hesperia and Insubria,
The fire in the ship, plague, and captivity,
Mercury in Aries, Saturn shall wither.

66
The prisoner escaped through great danger,
A little while after shall become great, his fortune being changed,
In the palace the people shall be caught,
And by a good sign the city shall be besieged.

67
The fair one shall fight with the forked nose,
In duel, and expel him out,
He shall re-establish the banished,
Putting the stronger of them in maritine places.

68
The endevours of the North shall be great,
Upon the ocean the gate shall be open,
The kingdom in the island shall be re-established,
London shall quake, for fear of sails discovered.

69

The French king, by the low-countrys right hand,
Seeing the discord of the great monarchy,
Upon three parts of it, will make his scepter to flourish,
Against the cap of the great hierarchy.

70

The dart of heaven shall make his circuit,
Some die speaking, a great execution,
The stone in the tree, the fierce people humbled,
Humane noise, a monster purged by expiation.

71

The banished persons shall come into Sicily,
To free the forrain nation from hunger,
In the dawning of the day the Celtes shall fail them,
Their life shall be preserved, the king shall submit to reason.

72

The French army shall be vexed in Italy,
On all sides fighting, and great loss,
The Romans run away, and thou France repulsed,
Near the Thesin, by Rubicon the fight shall be doubtful.

73

At the Fucin lake of the Benacle shore,
Near the Leman, at the port of Lorguion,
Born with three arms, a warlike image,
By three crowns to the great Endymion.

74

From Sens, from Autun they will come as far as the Rhone
To go further to the Pyrenean mountains,
The nation come from the March of Ancona,
By land and sea shall follow speedily after.

75

The noise of the unwonted bird having been heard,
Upon the cannon of the highest story,
The bushel of wheat shall rise so high,
That man will be eating his fellow man.

76

Lightning in Burgundy, with marvellous accidents,
Which could never have been done by art,
Of their senate sacriste being lamed,
Shall make known the business to the enemies.

77

Being repulsed with bows, fires, and pitch,
Cries and howlings shall be heard about midnight,
They shall get in through the broken walls,
The betrayers shall run away through the conduits.

78

The great Neptune of the deep of the sea
With Punic race and Gallic blood mixed.
The isles bled, because of the tardy rowing:
More harm will it do him than the ill-concealed secret.

79

The frizled and black beard by fighting,
Shall overcome the fierce and cruel nation,
The great Cheyren shall free from bands,
All the captives made by Selyne banner.

80

After the battle, the eloquency of the wounded man,
Within a little while shall procure a holy rest,
The great ones shall not be delivered,
But shall be left to their enemies will.

81

By fire from heaven the city shall be almost burnt,
The waters threatens another Deucalion,
Sardaigne shall be vexed by an African fleet,
After that libra shall have left her Phaeton.

82

Through hunger the prey will make the wolf prisoner,
The attacker then in extreme distress,
The heir having the last one before him,
The great one does not escape in the middle of the crowd.

83

The great trade of a great Lyon alter'd,
The most part turneth into its former ruine,
Shall become a prey to soldiers and reaped by wound,
In Mont-Jura, and Suaube great foggs.

84

Between campania, Sienna, Pisa and Ostia,
For six months and nine days there shall be no rain,
The strange language in Dalmatia's land,
Shall overrun, spoiling all the country.

85

The old plain beard under the severe statute,
Made at Lion upon the Celtique aigle,
The little great persevereth too far,
Noise of arms in the sky, the Ligustrian sea made red.

86

A fleet shall suffer shipwrack near the Adriatic sea,
The earthquake, a motion of the air cometh upon the land,
Egypt trembleth for fear of the Mahometan increase.
The herald surrendring shall be appointed to cry.

87

After that shall come out of the remote countries,
A German prince upon a gilded throne,
The slavery and waters shall meet,
The lady shall serve, her time no more worshipped.

88

The circumference of the ruinous building,
The seventh name shall be that of the fifth,
From a third, one greater, a warlike man,
Aries shall not preserve Paris nor Aix.

89

One day the two great masters shall be friends,
Their great power shall be increased,
The new land shall be in a flourishing condition,
The number shall be told to the bloody person.

90

By life and death the kingdom of Hungary shall be changed,
The law shall be more severe than the service,
Their great city shall be full of howling and crying,
Castor and Pollux shall be enemies in the list.

91

At the rising of the sun a great fire shall be seen,
Noise and light tending towards the North,
Within the round death and cries shall be heard,
Death by sword, fire, hunger watching for them.

92

A fire from heaven of a golden colour shall be seen,
Stricken by the high born, a wonderful case,
Great murder of mankind, the taking of the great Nephew,
Some dead looking, the proud one shall escape.

93

Near the Tiber, going towards Lybia,
A little before a great inundation,
The chief of the ship taken, thrown into the bilge,
And a castle and palace shall be burnt.

94

Great Po shall receive great harm by the French,
A vain terrour shall seize upon the maritine lion,
Infinite people shall go beyond sea,
Of which shall not escape a quarter of a million

95

The populous places shall be deserted,
A great division to obtain fields,
Kingdoms given to prudents incapable,
When the great bothers shall die by dissention.

96

A burning shall be seen by night in heaven,
Near the end and beginning of the Rhone,
Famine, sword, too late succours shall be provided,
Persia shall come against Macedonia.

97

Roman pontiff take heed to come near,
To the city watered with two rivers,
Thou shall spit there thy blood,
Thou and thine, when the rose shall blossom.

98

He that shall have his face bloody,
With the blood of the victim near to be sacrificed,
The sun coming into leo shall be an augury by presage,
That then he shall be put to death for his confidence.

99

The Roman country in which the augur did interpret,
Shall be too much vexed by the French nation,
But the Celtique nation shall fear the hour,
The Northwind had driven the navy in too far.

100

In the islands shall be so horrid tumults,
That nothing shall be heard but a warlike surprise,
So great shall be the insult of the robbers,
That every one shall shelter himself under the great league.

CENTURY III

1
After the fight and sea battle,
The great Neptune in his highest Steeple,
The red adversary shall wax pale for fear,
Putting the great ocean in a fright.

2
The divine word shall give to the substance,
Heaven and earth, and gold hid in the mystical milk,
Body, soul, spirit, having all power,
As well under his feet, as in the heavenly seat.

3
Mars and Mercury, and silver joyned together,
Towards the South a great drought,
In the bottome of Asia shall be an earthquake,
Corinth and Ephesus shall then be in perplexity.

4
When the want of the luminaries shall be near,
Not being far distant one from another,
Cold, drought, danger towards the frontiers,
Even where the oracle had his beginning.

5
Near the eclipses of the two great luminaries,
Which shall happen between April and March,
O what a dearth! but two great ones bountiful,
By land and sea shall succour them on all sides.

6
Into a close church the lightning shall fall,
The citizens shall be distressed in their fort,
Horses, oxen, men, the water shall touch the wall,
By hunger, thirst, down shall come the worst provided.

7
The runaways, fire of heaven upon the pikes,
A fight near hand, the ravens sporting,
They cry from the land, succours o heavenly powers
When near the walls shall be the fighting men.

8
The Cimbres joyned with their neighbours,
Shall come to depopulate almost all Spain,
People gathered from Guienne and Limousin,
Shall be in league with them, and keep them company.

9

Bourdeaux, Rouen, and La Rochelle joyned together,
Will range about upon the great ocean,
English Brittans, and Flemings joyned together,
Shall drive them away as far as Rouane.

10

Of blood and famine, what a great calamity!
Seven times is ready to come upon the sea coast,
Monaco by hunger, the place taken, captivity,
The great one carried away, croc, shut up in a cage.

11

Armies shall fight in the air a great while,
The tree shall fall in the middle of the city,
Vermin, scabs, sword, fire-brand in the face,
When the Monaco of Adria shall fall.

12

Because of the swelling of the Ebro, Po, Tagus, Tiber and Rhine
And because of the pond of Geneva and Arezzo,
The two great chiefs and cities of the Garonne,
Taken, dead, drowned: human booty divided.

13

By lightning shall gold and silver be melted in the arch,
Of two prisoners one shall eat up the other,
The greatest of the city shall be laid down,
When the navy that was drowned shall swim.

14

By the bow of the valliant men,
Of weak France, by the unfortunate father,
Honours, riches, labour in his old age,
For having believed the councel of a nice man.

15
Heart, vigour, and glory shall change the kingdom,
In all points, having an adversary against it,
Then shall France overcome childhood by death,
A great regent shall then be more adversary to it.

16
An English prince Mars hath his heart from heaven,
Will follow his prosperous fortune,
Of two duels one shall pierce the gall,
Being hated of him, and beloved of his mother.

17
Mount Aventine shall be seen to burn in the night,
The heaven shall be darkned upon a sudden in Flanders,
When the monarch shall expel his Nephew,
Then churchmen shall commit scandals.

18
After a pretty long rain of milk,
In many places of Reims the lightning shall fall,
O what a bloody fight is making ready near them,
Father and son, both kings, shall not dare to come near.

19
In Luca it shall rain blood and milk,
A little before the change of the magistrate,
A great plague, war, hunger and thirst shall be seen,
A great way off, where their prince ruler shall die.

20
Through the countries of the great river betis,
Far from Iberia, in the kingdom of Granada,
Crosses beaten back by Mahometan people,
One of Corduba shall at last betray the country.

21
In the Conca by the Adriatic sea
There will appear a horrible fish,
Having a mans face, and a fishes body,
Which shall be taken without a hook.

22
Six days shall the assault be given to the city,
A great and fierce battle shall be fought,
Three shall surrender it and be pardoned,
The rest shall be put to fire and sword, cut and slasht.

23
If France goeth beyond the Ligurian sea,
Thou shall see thy self inclosed with islands and seas,
Mahomet, against thee besides the Adriatic sea,
Of horses and asses thou shalt gnaw the bones.

24
From the undertaking great confusion,
Loss of people and innumerable treasury,
Thou oughtest not yet to tend that way,
France endeavour to remember my saying.

25
He that shall obtain the kingdom of Navarre,
When Sicily and Naples shall be joyned,
Bigorre and landes then by Foix shall beheld
Of one who shall too much be joyned to Spain.

26
Some kings and princes shall set up idols,
Divinations and hollow raised divinators,
Victim with gilded horns, and set with azur and mother of pearl
The looking into the entrals shall be interpreted.

27

A Libian prince being powerful in the West,
The French shall love so much the Arabian Language,
That he being a learned man shall condescend,
To have the Arabian tongue translated into French.

28

One weak in lands and of poor kindred,
By thrusting, and peace shall attain to the empire,
Long time shall reign a young woman,
Such as in a reign was never a worse.

29

The two nephews brought up in divers places,
A sea fight, fathers fallen to the earth,
They shall came highly educated, and expert in arms,
To avenge the injury, their enemies shall fall down under them.

30

He who in wrestling and Martial affairs,
Had carried the prize before his better,
By night six shall abuse him in his bed,
Being naked, and without harness, he shall suddenly be surprised.

31

In the fields of Media, Arabia, and Armenia,
Two great armies shall meet thrice,
Near the shore of Araxes, the people
Of great suleiman shall fall down.

32

The great grave of the Aquitanick people,
Shall come near Tuscany,
When Mars shall be in the German corner,
And in the territory of the Mantuan people.

33

In the city wherein the wolf shall go,
Near that place the enemies shall be,
An army of strangers shall spoil a great country,
The friends shall go over the mountains of the Alpe.

34

When the eclipse of the sun shall be
At noon day, the monster shall be seen,
It shall be interperted otherways,
Then for a dearth, because no body hath provided against it.

35

Out of the deepest part of the West of Europe,
From poor people a young child shall be born,
Who with his tongue shall seduce many people,
His fame shall increase in the Eastern kingdom

36

One buried, not dead, but apoplectical,
Shall be found to have eaten up his hands,
When the city shall blame the heretical man,
Who as they thought had changed their laws.

37

Before the assault the prayer shall be said,
An eagle shall take a kite, they shall be deceived by an ambush.
The ancient wall shall be beaten down with cannons,
By fire and blood, few shall have quarter.

38

The French nation, and another nation,
Being over the mountains, shall die, and be taken,
In a month contrary to them, and near the vintage,
By the lords agreed together.

39

The seven shall agree together within three months,
To conquer the Apennine Alpes,
But the tempest, and coward Genoese,
Shall sink them into sudden ruines.

40

The great Theatre shall be raised up again,
The dice being cast, and the nest spread,
The first shall too much in glass.
Beaten down by bows, who long before were split.

41

Crook-back shall be chosen by the council,
A more hideous monster I never saw upon earth.
The flying blow shall put out one of his eyes,
The Ttraitor to the king, shall be admited as faithful.

42

A child shall be born with two teeth in his mouth.
It shall rain stones in Tuscany,
A few years after there shall be neither wheat nor barley
To feed those that shall faint for hunger.

43

People that live about the Tar, Lot, and Garonne,
Take heed to go over the Apennine mountains,
Your grave is near Rome and Ancona,
The black frisled hair shall dress a trophy of you.

44

When the beast familiar to mankind,
After great labour, and leaping shall come to speak,
The lightning shall be so hurtful to a virgin,
That she shall be taken from the earth, and suspended in the air.

45

The five strangers having come into the church,
The blood shall prophane the ground,
It shall be a hard example to those of Thoulouse,
Concerning one that came to break their laws.

46

The heaven foretelleth concerning the city of Plancus,
By famous clerks, and fixed stars,
That the time of her sudden change is near hand,
Neither because of her goodness, or wickedness.

47

The old monarch being expelled out of his kingdom,
Shall go into the East to get succours,
For fear of the crosses he shall fold up his colours,
He shall go into Mitylene by sea and land.

48

Seven hundred prisoners shall be tied together,
To murder half of them, the lot being cast,
The next hope shall come quickly,
And not so quickly, but fifteen shall be dead before.

49

French kingdom thou shalt be much changed,
The empire is translated in another place,
Thou shalt be put into other manners and laws,
Rouen and Chartres shall do the worse they can to thee.

50

The Commonwealth of the great city,
With great harshness shall not consent,
That the king should go out being summoned by a trumpet,
The ladder shall be put to the wall, and the city repent.

51

Paris conspireth to commit a great murder,
Blois will cause it to come to pass,
Those of Orleans will set up their head again,
Angers, Troyes, Langres will commit a misdeed against them.

52

In campania shall be so long a rain,
And in Apulia so great a drought,
The cock shall see the eagle with his wing disordered,
And by the lion brought to extremity.

53

When the great one shall carry the prize,
Of Nuremberg, of Augsburg, and those of Basle,
By Agrippina the chief of Frankfort shall be taken,
They shall go through Flanders as far as France.

54

One of the greatest shall run away into Spain,
That shall cause a wound to bleed long,
Leading armies over the high mountains,
Destroying all, and afterwards shall Raign.

55

In the year that one eye shall reign in France,
The court shall be in a very hard trouble,
The great one of Blois shall kill his friend,
The kingdom shall be in an ill case, and double doubt.

56

Montauban, Nismes, Avignon and Beziers,
Plague, lightning and hail at the end of March,
The bridge of Paris, the wall of Lyon, and Monpelier, shall fall,
From six hundred and seven score, three parts.

57

Seven times you shall see the English to change,
Died in blood, in two hundred ninety year,
Not France, by the German support,
Aries doubleth his Bastarnan pole.

58

Near the Rhine, out of the Norick mountains,
Shall be born a great one, though too late come,
Who shall defend the Polonians and Hungarians,
So that it shall not be known what is become of him.

59

A Barbarian empire shall be usurped by a third person,
Who shall put to death the greatest part of his Kindred,
By death of old age, the fourth shall be stricken by him,
For fear that blood should not die by blood.

60

Through all Asia shall be a great proscription,
Yea in Mysia, Lydia, and Pamphilia,
Blood shall be spilled by the debauchness
Of a young black man, full of felony.

61

The great troop and sect wearing a cross,
Shall rise up in Mesopotamia,
Near the next river shall be a light company,
Which shall hold that law for enemy.

62

Near the Duero closed by the Cyrenian sea,
Shall come to pierce the great Pyrenean mountains,
The shorter hand and his pierced glose,
Shall in Carcassone lead his plot.

63

The Roman power shall be quite put down,
His great neighbour shall follow his steps,
Secret and civil hatreds and quarrels,
Shall stop the buffoons folly.

64

The head of Persia shall fill a great Olchade,
A fleet of galleys against the Mahometan nation,
From Parthia and Media they shall come to plunder the Cyclades,
A long rest shall be on the Jonique port.

65

When the sepulcher of the great Roman shall be found,
The next day after a pope shall be elected,
Who shall not be much approved by the senate,
Poisoned, his blood in the sacred scyphe.

66

The great bailif of Orleans shall be put to death,
By one of a revengeful blood,
He shall not die of a deserved death, nor by chance,
But the disease of being tied hand and foot, hath made him prisoner.

67

A new sect of Philosophers shall rise,
Despising death, gold, honours and riches,
They shall be near the mountains of Germany,
They shall have abundance of others to support and follow them.

68

A people of Spain and Italy without a Head,
Shall die, being overcome in the Cheronese,
Their saying shall be betrayed by a light folly,
The blood shall swim all over at random.

69

A great army led by a young man,
Shall yield it self in the hands of the enemies,
But the old man born at the sign of the half-hog,
Shall cause Chalon and Mascon to be friends.

70

Great Britany comprehended in England,
Shall suffer so great an inundation by waters,
The new league of Ausone shall make wars,
So that they shall stand against them.

71

Those in the islands that have been long besieged,
Shall take vigour and force against their enemies,
Those without shall die for hunger; being overcome,
They shall be put in greater famine then they were before.

72

The good old man shall be buried alive,
Near the great river by a false suspicion,
The new old one made noble by his riches,
The gold of his ransom shall be taken in the way.

73

When the lame man shall attain to the kingdom,
He shall have a bastard for his near competitor,
He, and his kingdom shall be so scabby,
That before he be cured it will be late.

74

Naples, Florence, Fayenza, and Imola,
Shall be put into so much distress,
For being complaisant to the unhappy one of Nola,
Who was complained of for having mocked his superiour.

75

Pau, Verona, Vicenza, Saragossa,
Shall be hit by the sword, the country shall be moist with blood,
So great a plague and so vehement shall come,
That though the succours be near, the remedy shall be far off.

76

In Germany shall divers sects arise,
Coming very near the happy paganism,
The heart captivated and small receivings,
Shall open the gate to pay the true tithes.

77

The third climat comprehended under Aries,
In the year 1700. the twenty seven of October,
The king of Persia shall be taken by those of Egypt,
Battle, death, loss, a great shame to the christians.

78

The chief of Scotland with six of Germany,
Shall be taken prisoners by seamen of the East,
They shall go through the Calpre and Spain,
And shall be made a present in Persia to the new fearful king.

79

The great bawler proud without shame,
Shall be elected governor of the army,
The stoutness of his competitor,
The bridge being broken, the city shall faint for fear.

80

The worthy one chased out of the English realm,
The adviser through angur put to the fire:
His adherents will go so low to efface themselves
That the bastard will be half received.

81

The great shameless, audacious bawler,
He will be elected governor of the army:
The boldness of his contention,
The bridge broken, the city faint from fear.

82

Frejus, Antibes, towns around Nice,
They will be thoroughly devastated by sea and by land:
The locusts by land and by sea the wind propitious,
Captured, dead, bound, pillaged without law of war.

83

The long hairs of Celtic Gaul
Accompanied by foreign nations,
They will make captive the people of Aquitaine,
For succumbing to their designs.

84

The great city shall be made very desolate.
Not one of the Inhabitants shall be left in it,
Wall, sex, church, and virgin ravished,
By sword, fire, plague, cannon, people shall die.

85

The city shall be taken by cheat and deceit,
By the means of a fair young one caught in it,
Assault shall be given, Raubine near Laude,
He, and all shall die, for having deceived.

86

A chief man of Ausone shall go into Spain
By sea, he shall stay at Marseilles,
He shall languish a great while before his death,
After his death great wonders shall be seen.

87

French fleet do not come near unto Corsica,
Much less to Sardinia, thou shalt repent of it,
All of you shall die frustrate of the help Greigne,
Blood shall swim, being captive thou shalt not believe me.

88

There shall come from Barcelona by sea so great a fleet,
That Marseilles shall quake for fear,
The islands shall be seized, the help by sea shut up,
Thy traitor shall swim to land.

89

At that time Cyprus shall be frustrated
Of its succours, of those of the Aegean sea,
Old ones slaughtered: but by speeches and supplications,
Their king shall be seducted, and the queen more wronged.

90

The great Satyr and Tyger of Hircania,
Shall be a gift presented to those of the ocean,
An Admiral of a fleet shall come out of Carmania,
One who will take land at the 'Tyrren Phocaean.'

91

The tree that had been long dead and withered,
In one night shall grow green again,
His king shall be sick, his prince shall have his foot tied,
Being feared by his enemies, he shall make his sails to rebound.

92

The world near the last period,
Saturn will come back again late:
Empire transferred towards the dusky nation,
The eye plucked out by the Goshawk at Narbonne.

93

In Avignon all the chief of the empire,
Shall stay, by reason of Paris being desolate,
'Tricast' will hold the anger of Hannibal:
Lion by change shall be ill comforted.

94

For five hundred years no account shall be made,
Of him who was the ornament of his time:
Then on a sudden he shall give so great a light,
That for that age he shall make them to be most contented.

95

We shall see the Morish law to decline,
After which, another more seducing shall arise,
Boristhenes shall be the first that shall fall,
By gifts and tongue that law shall be most seducing.

96

The chief of Fossan shall have his throat cut,
By the leader of the hunt and greyhond,
The fact committed by those of the Tarpeian mountain,
Saturn being in leo the 13. of February.

97

A new law shall occupy a new country,
Towards Syria, Judea and Palestina,
The great Barbarian empire shall fall down,
Before the moon completes it cycle.

98

Two royal bothers shall war so much one against the other,
That the war between them shall be mortal,
Each of them shall seize upon strong places,
Their quarrel shall be concerning kingdom and life.

99

In the meadow fields of Alein and Varneigre,
Of the mountain Lebron near the Durance,
Armies on both sides, the fight shall be so sharp,
That Mesopotamia shall be wanting in France.

100

He that is the least honoured among the French,
Shall be conqueror of the man that was his enemy,
Strength and terrour shall in a moment be tried,
When the envious shall be killed with an arrow.

CENTURY IV

1
There shall be a remnant of blood unspilt,
Venice shall seek for succours,
After having long waited for it,
The city shall be surrendred at the first sound of the trumpet.

2
By reason of a death, France shall undertake a journey,
They shall have a fleet at sea, and march towards the Pyrenes,
Spain shall be in trouble by an army,
Some of the greatest ladies in France carried away

3
From Arras and Bourges many colours of black men shall come,
A greater number of Gascons shall go on foot,
Those along the Rhosne shall let Spain blood,
Near the mountain where Saguntus is seated.

4
The considerable prince vexed, complaineth and quarelleth,
Concerning rapes and plunderings done by the cocks and libiques
Great trouble by land, by sea infinite sails,
Italy alone shall drive away the French.

5
The cross shall have peace, under an accomplished divine word,
Spain and France shall be united together,
A great battle near hand, and a most sharp fight,
No heart so stout but shall tremble.

6
By the new clothes after the find is made,
There shall be malice, plotting and machination,
He shall die the first that shall make trial of it,
Under colour of Venice, shall be a conspiracy.

7
The younger son of the great and hated prince,
Being twenty years, old shall have a great touch of leprosie,
His mother shall die for grief, very sad and lean,
And he shall die of the disease loose flesh.

8
The great city shall be taken by a sudden assault,
Being surprised by night, the watch being beaten,
The court of guard and watch of Saint Quentin
Shall be killed, and the gates broken.

9
The chief of the camp in the middle of the crowd,
Shall be wounded with an arrow through both his thighs,
When Geneva being in tears and distress,
SWill be betrayed by Lausanne and the Swiss.

10
The young prince being falsely accused,
Shall put the camp in trouble, and in quarrele,
The chief shall be murdered by the tumult,
The scepter shall be appeased, and after cure the kings-evil.

11
He that shall be covered with a great cloak,
Shall be induced to commit some great fact,
The twelve red ones shall soil the tablecloth,
Under murder, murder shall be committed.

12
The greatest camp being in disorder, shall be routed,
And shall be pursued not much after,
The army shall incamp again, and the troops set in order,
Then afterwards, they shall be wholly driven out of France.

13
News being brought of a great loss,
The report divulged, the camp shall be astonished,
Troops being united and revolted,
The double Phalanx shall forsake the great one.

14
The sudden death of the chief man,
Shall cause a change, and put another in the sovereignty,
Soon, late come to so high a degree, in a low age,
So that by land and sea he must be feared.

15
Whence one thought to make famine to come,
Thence shall come the fulness,
The eye of the sea through a doggish covetousness,
For the one the other will give oil and wheat.

16
The free city from a free one shall become slave,
And of the banished and dreamers shall be a retreat,
The king changed in mind, shall not be so froward to them.
Of one hundred they shall become more than a thousand.

17
There shall be a change at Beaune, Nuis, Chalons, Dijon,
The duke going about to raise taxes,
The merchant near the river shall see the tail
Of a fish, having the bill of a cormorant: the door shall be shut.

18

The most learned in the celestial sciences,
Shall be found fault with, by ignorant princes.
Punished by proclamation, chased away as wicked,
And put to death where they shall be found.

19

Before Rouen the siege laid by the Insubrians,
By land and sea the passages shut up:
By Hainaut and Flanders, by Ghent and those of Liege
Through cloaked gifts they will ravage the shores.

20

Peace and plenty shall not be long praised,
All the time of his reign the flower de Luce shall be deserted,
Bodies shall die by water, earth shall be brought,
Hoping vainly to be there Buried.

21

The change shall be very hard,
The city and country shall gain by the change,
A high prudent heart shall be put in, the unworthy expelled,
Sea, land, people shall change its condition.

22

The great army that shall be rejected,
In a moment shall be wanted by the king.
The faith promised a far off shall be broken,
So that he shall be left naked in a pitiful case.

23

The legion in the maritine fleet,
Calcineth magnes, shall burn brimstone and pitch,
The long rest of the secure place,
They shall seek port Selyn, but fire shall consume them.

24

Under ground shall be heard the fained voice of a holy dame,
An humane flame to see a divine one,
Shall cause the ground to be died with the sisters blood,
And the holy temples to be destroyed by the wicked

25

The celestial bodies that are always visible to the eye,
Shall be darkened for these reasons,
The body with the forehead sense and head invincible.
Diminishing the sacred prayers.

26

The great swarm of bees shall rise,
And it shall not be known whence they come,
Towards the ambush so the Jay shall be under a vines,
A city shall be betray'd by five tongues not naked.

27
Salon, Mansol, Tarascon, Desex, the arche,
Where to this day standeth the pyramid,
Shall come to deliver the prince of Denmark,
A shameful ransom shall be paid in the temple of Artemis.

28
When Venus shall be covered by the sun,
Under the splendor of it shall be an occult form,
Mercury in the fire shall discover them,
And by a warlike rumor shall be provoked.

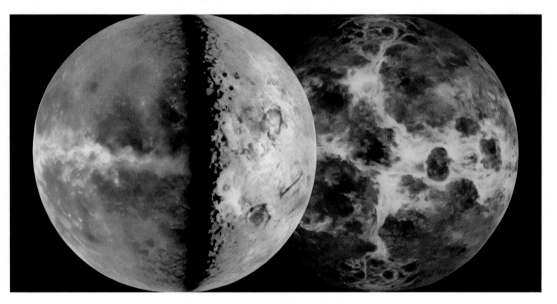

29
The sun shall be hid and eclipsed by Mercury,
And shall not be set but for the second heaven,
Hermes shall be made a prey to Vulcan,
And after that the sun shall be seen pure, shining and yellow.

30
The moon will not have the sun above eleven times,
Then both shall be encreased and lessened in degree,
And put so low, that a little gold shall be sowed up,
So that after hunger and plague, the secret shall be discovered.

31
The moon at full by night upon the high mount,
The new sage with one onely brain hath seen it,
Invited by his disciples to become immortal,
His eyes to the South, conclusion, his hands and body to the fire.

32
In places and times, flesh shall give place to fish,
The common law shall be made against it,
The old man shall stand fast, then being taken away
Loving of Everything in Common put far behind.

33
Jupiter being more joyned to Venus then to the moon,
Appearing in a full whiteness,
Venus being hid under the whiteness of Neptune,
Stricken by Mars through the ingraved branch.

34
The great one brought prisoner from a far country,
And chained with gold, shall be presented to the king Chyren,
Being then at Ausone. Milan shall loose the war.
And all its host shall be put to fire and sword.

35
The fire being put out, the virgins shall betray,
The greatest part of the new troup,
Gunpowder, lance, shall keep only the kings,
In Hetruria and Corsica by night throats shall be cut.

36
The new plays shall be set up again in France,
After the victory obtained in Piemont,
Mountains of Spain, the great ones tied, carried away,
Romania and Spain shall quake for fear.

37
The French by leaping shall go over the mountains,
And shall seize upon the great mount of the Savoyard,
He shall cause his army to go to the furthermost,
Genoa, and Monaco shall set out their red fleet.

38
While the duke shall busie the king and the queen,
A great man of Constantinople shall be prisoner in Samothracia,
Before the assault one shall eat up the other,
Rebours shod shall trace one by the blood.

39
The Rhodians shall ask for succours,
Being forsaken by the neglect of her heirs,
The Arabian empire shall slack his course,
By the means of Spain the case shall be mended.

40
The fortresses of the besieged shut up,
Through gunpowder sunk into the abyss:
The traitors will all be stowed away alive,
Never did such a pitiful schism happen to the sextons.

41
Female sex captive as a hostage
Will come by night to deceive the guards:
The chief of the army deceived by her language
Will abandon her to the people, it will be pitiful to see.

42
Geneve and Langres by those of Chartres and Dole,
And by one of Grenoble captive at Montlimar,
Seisset, Lausanne by a fraudulent deceit,
Shall betray them for thirty pounds weight of gold.

43
There shall be heard in the air noise of weapons,
And in that same year the divines shall be enemies,
They shall unjustly put down the holy laws,
And by the thunder and the war true believers shall die.

44
Two large ones of Mende, of Rodez and Milhau
Cahors, Limoges, Castres bad week
By night the entry shall be from Bourdeaux an insult,
Through Perigort at the ringing of the bell.

45

By a battle the king shall forsake his kingdom,
The greatest commander, shall fail in time of need,
They shall be killed and routed, few shall escape,
They shall be cut off, one only shall be left for a witness.

46

The fact shall be defended excellently well
Tours beware of thy approaching ruine,
London and Nantes by Reims shall stand upon their defence,
Do not go further in foggy weather.

47

The wild black one, after he shall have tryed,
His bloody hand by fire, sword, bended bows,
All the people shall be so frighted,
To see the greatest hanged by the neck and feet.

48

The plain about Bourdeaux fruitful and spacious,
Shall produce so many hornets and so many grasshoppers,
That the light of the sun shall be darkened,
They shall crap all, a great plague shall come from them.

49

Before the people blood shall be spilt,
Who shall not come far from the high heaven,
But it shall not be heard of for a great while,
The spirit of one shall come to witness it.

50

Libra shall see Spain to reign,
And have the monarchy of heaven and earth,
No body shall see the forces of Asia to perish,
Till seven have kept the hierarchy successively.

51

A duke being earnest in the pursute of his enemy
Shall come in, hindering the phalanx,
Hastened on foot shall follow them so close,
That the day of the battle shall be near Ganges.

52

In a besieged city, men and women being upon the walls,
The enemies without, the governor ready to surrender,
The wind shall be strong against the soldiers,
They shall be driven away by lime, dust, and ashes.

53

The runnaways and banished men being recalled,
Fathers and sons garnishing the high wells,
The cruel father and his retinue shall be suffocated,
His son being worse, shall be drowned in the well.

54

Of the name that a French king never was,
There was never a lightning so much feared,
Italy shall tremble, Spain and the English,
He shall be much taken with women strangers.

55

When the crow upon a tower made of brick,
For seven hours shall do nothing but cry,
Death shall be foretold, and the statue died with blood,
Tyrant shall be murdered, and the people pray to the gods.

56

After the victory got over a raging tongue,
The mind that was tempted, shall be in tranquility and rest,
The bloody conqueror by battle shall make a speech,
And roast the tongue, the flesh, and the bones.

57

Ignorant envy being supported by the great king,
Shall talk of prohibiting the writtings,
His wife no wife, being tempted by another,
Shall more then they two prevail by crying.

58

Burning sun shall be poured into the throat,
This human blood shall wet the Hetrurian ground,
The chief pale of water, shall lead his son to Spin,
A captive lady shall be carried into the Turkish land.

59

Two besieged, being in a burning heat,
Shall die for thirst, want of two bowls full,
The fort being filed, an old doting man,
Shall show to the Genoese the way to Nizza

60

The seven children left in hostage,
The third will come to slaughter his child:
Because of his son two will be pierced by the point,
Genoa, Florence, he will come to confuse them.

61

The seven children being left in hostage,
The third shall come to kill his child,
Two by their sons shall be run through,
Genoa and Florence shall second them.

62

A colonel deviseth a plot by his ambition,
He shall seize upon the best part of the army,
Against his prince he shall have a fained invention,
And shall be discovered under the harbour of the vine.

63

The Celtic army against the mountaineers,
Those who will be learned and able in bird-calling:
Peasants will soon work fresh presses,
All hurled on the sword's edge.

64

The guilty, in a citizens habit,
Shall come to tempt the king concerning his offence,
Fifteen soldiers the most part country men,
The last shall be his life, and the best part of his estate.

65

After that the desertor of the great fort,
Shall have forsaken his place,
His adversary shall do so great feats,
That the emperor, shall soon be condemned to death.

66

Under the fained colour of seven shaven heads,
Shall divers spies be framed,
Wells and fountains shall be sprinkled with poison,
In the fort of Genoa shall be humane devourers.

67

In the year that Saturn and Mars shall be fiery,
The air shall be very dry, in many countrys,
By secret fires, many places shall be burnt with heat,
There shall be scarcity of rain, hot winds, wars, in-roads.

68

In a year that is to come shortly, and not far from Venus,
The two greatest ones of Asia and Affrica,
Shall be said to come from the Rhine and Ister,
Crying, and tears shall be at Malta and in the Ligurian shore.

69

The banished shall keep the great city,
The citizens being dead, murdered and expelled,
Those of Aquileia shall promise to Parma,
To shew the entrance by unknown paths.

70

Near the great Pyrenean mountains,
One shall raise a great army against the eagle,
Veins shall be opened, forces driven out,
So that the chief shall be driven as far as the Pau.

71

Instead of the bride, the maid shall be killed,
The murder shall be a great fault, none shall be surviving,
In the well they shall be drowned with their cloaths,
The bride shall be extinguished by an high Aconite.

72

The Artomiques through agen and Lectoure,
Shall keep their parliament at Saint Fœlix,
These of Bazas shall come in an unhappy hour,
To seize upon Condon and Marsan speedily.

73

The great nephew by force shall provoke,
The sin committed by the pusillanimous heart,
Ferrara and Ast shall make tryal of the duke,
When the pantomime shall be in the evening.

74

Those of lake Geneva and of Macon:
All assembled against those of Aquitaine:
Many Germans many more Swiss,
They will be routed along with those of 'Humane.'

75

Ready to fight one will desert,
The chief adversary will obtain the victory:
The rear guard will make a defense,
The faltering ones dead in the white territory.

76

The people of agen by those of Perigord
Will be vexed, holding as far as the Rhone:
The union of Gascons and Bigorre
To betray the temple, the priest giving his sermon.

77

Selyn being monarch, Italy shall be in peace,
Kingdoms shall be united, a Christian king of the world,
Dying, shall desire to be buried in the country of Blois,
After he shall have driven the pirates from the sea.

78

The great army belonging to the Civil war,
Having found by night Parma possessed by Strangers,
Shall kill seventy nine in the town,
And put all the Strangers to the sword.

79

Royal blood run away from Monheurt, Marsan, Aiguillon,
The landes shall be full of Bourdeloir,
Navarre, Bigorre, shall have points and Pricks.
Being deep in hunger, they shall devour the Cork and Akorns.

80

Near the great river, a great pit, earth digged out,
In fifteen parts the water shall be divided,
The city taken, fire, blood, cries, fighting,
And the greatest part involving the colosseum.

81

A bridge of boats shall suddenly be made,
To pass over the army of the great Belgian prince,
In deep places, and not far from Bruxelles,
Being gone over, there shall be seven cut with a pike.

82

A great troop gathered, shall come from Sclavonia,
The old destroyer shall ruine a city,
He shall see his Romania very desolate,
And after that, shall not be able to quench that great flame.

83

In a fight by night, the valliant captain,
Being vanquished shall run away, overcome by few,
His people being moved, shall make no small mutiny,
His own son shall besiege him.

84

A great man of Auxerre shall die very miserably,
Being expelled by those that have been under him,
Bound with chains, and after that with a strong cable,
In the year that Mars, Venus, and sol shall be in a conjunction in the Summer.

85

The white Coal shall be expelled by the black one,
He shall be made prisoner, carried in a dung-cart,
His feet twisted upon a black camel,
Then the youngest, shall suffer the hobby to have more thread.

86

In the year that Saturn in Aquarius shall be in conjunction
With sol, the king being strong and powerful,
Shall be received and Anointed at Rheines and Aix,
After conquest he shall murder innocent persons.

87

A king's son learned in many languages,
Different from his senior in the realm:
His handsome father understood by the greater son,
He will cause his principal adherent to perish.

88

Anthony by name great by the filthy fact
Of lousiness wasted to his end:
One who will want to be desirous of lead,
Passing the port he will be immersed by the elected one.

89

Thirty of London shall secretly conspire,
Against their king, upon the bridge the plot shall be made,
These satellites shall taste of death,
A fair king elected, native of Frisia.

90

The two armies shall not be able to joyn by the walls,
At that instant Milan and Thesin shall tremble,
Hunger, thirst, and fear shall so seize upon them,
They shall not have a bit of meat, bread, nor victuals.

91

A French duke compelled to fight a duel,
The ship of mole shall not come near Monaco,
Wrongfully accused shall have a perpetual prison,
His son shall endeavour to reign before his death.

92

The head cut off the valliant captain
Shall be thrown down before his adversary,
His body hanged at the sails yard,
Confused, they shall fly with oars against the wind.

93

A Serpent shall be seen near the royal bed,
By a lady in the night, the dogs shall not bark,
Then shall be born in France a prince so royal,
Come from heaven all the princes shall see it.

94

Two great bothers shall be driven from Spain,
The elder of them shall be overcome under the Pyrenean mountains
Bloody sea, Rhosne, Blood Leman of Germany,
Narbon, Bliterre of Agath polluted.

95

The kingdom being left to two, they shall keep it but a little while,
Three years and seven months being past, they shall make war,
The two vestals shall rebel against them,
The youngest shall be conqueror in the Armorick country.

96

The eldest sister of the Brittain island,
Shall be born fifteen years before her bother,
By what is promised her, and help of the truth,
She shall succeed in the kingdom of libra.

97

When Mercury, Mars and Venus shall retrograde,
The Line of the great monarch shall be wanting,
He shall be elected by the Lusitanians near Pactole,
And shall reign in peace a good while.

98

The Albanians shall pass through Rome,
By the means of Langres covered with half helmets,
Marquess and duke shall spare no man,
Fire, blood, smallpox no water the crops to fail.

99

The valliant eldest son of the daughter of the king,
Shall beat back so far those of Flanders,
That he will cast lightnings, o how many in such orders
Little and far, after shall go deep in Spain.

100

Fire shall fall from the skies on the kings palace,
When Mars's light shall be eclipsed,
A great war shall be for seven months, people shall die by witchcraft.
Rouen, and Eureux shall not be wanting to the king.

CENTURY V

1

Before the coming of the ruine of Flanders,
Two shall discourse together in the church,
Dagger in the heart by one, on horse-back and spurring,
Without noise they shall bury the great one.

2

Seven conspirators at a banquet shall make their iron glister
Against three, out of a ship:
One shall carry the two fleets to the great one,
When in the evil the last shall shoot him in the forehead.

3

The Successor to the dukedom shall come,
Far beyond the Tuscane sea,
A French branch shall hold Florence
In its Lap, to which the sea-frog shall agree.

4

The great mastif being driven from the city,
Shall be angry at the strange alliance,
After he shall have hunted the stag in the fields,
The wolf, and the bear shall defie one another.

5

Under the fained shadow of freeing people from slavery,
He shall usurpe the people and city for himself;
He shall do worse by the deceit of a young whore,
For he shall be betrayed in the field reading a false proem.

69

6

The augur shall come to put his hand upon the kings head,
And pray for the peace of Italy,
In the left hand he shall change the scepter,
Of a king he shall become a peaceful emperor.

7

The bones of the Triumuir shall be found out,
When they shall seek for a deep and ænigmatical treasure,
Those there about shall not be in rest,
This concavity shall be marble and metallic Lead.

8

The fire shall be left burning, the dead man shall be hid,
Within the globes terrible and fearful,
By night the fleet shall shoot against the city,
The city shall be on fire, the enemy shall be favourable unto it.

9

The great arch demolished down to its base,
By a captain that is a prisoner, the friend shall be anticipated,
One shall be born of a lady with a hoary face and forehead,
Then by craft shall a duke be put to death.

10

A general of Flanders wounded in battle,
Near a cellar, seeing death to overthrow his people,
Being much oppressed with blood, wounds and enemies,
Is succoured by four unknown.

11

The sea will not be passed over safely by those of the sun,
Those of Venus will hold all Africa:
Saturn will no longer occupy their realm,
And the Asiatic part will change.

12

To near the lake of Geneva will it be conducted,
By the foreign maiden wishing to betray the city:
Before its murder at Augsburg the great suite,
And those of the Rhine will come to invade it.

13

With great fury the Roman Belgian king
Will want to vex the barbarian with his phalanx:
Fury gnashing, he will chase the African people
From the Pannonias to the pillars of Hercules.

14

Saturn and Mars being in leo, Spain shall be captive,
By a Lybian general taken in the battle,
Near Malta, an heirse shall be taken alive,
And the Roman scepter shall be strucken by the cock.

15

In sailing a pope shall be taken captive;
After which, shall be a great uproar amongst the clergy,
A second absent elected, consumeth his goods,
His favourite bastard shall be killed.

16

The Sabaean tear no longer at its high price,
Turning human flesh into ashes through death,
At the isle of Pharos disturbed by the crusaders,
When at Rhodes will appear a hard phantom.

17

By night the king passing near an Alley,
He of Cyprus and chief of the war,
The king having missed the hand, runneth away along by the Rhone,
The conspirators shall put him to death there.

18

The unhappy being overcome, shall die for grief,
His Victrix shall celebrate the Hecatomb,
The former law and free edict shall be brought again,
The wall and seventh prince shall go to the grave.

19

The great golden royal, being increased with copper,
The agreement being broken by a young man, there shall be open war,
People afflicted by the loss of a general lamented,
The ground shall be covered with barbarous blood.

20

The great army will pass beyond the Alps,
Shortly before will be born a monster scoundrel:
Prodigious and sudden he will turn
The great Tuscan to his nearest place.

21

By the death of the Latin monarch,
Those that he shall have succoured in his reign.
The fire shall shine, the booty shall be divided,
The stout comers in shall be put to publick death.

22

Before the great one has given up the ghost at Rome,
The army of strangers shall be put into a great fright,
By Squadrons the ambush shall be near Parma.
After that, the two red ones shall make good cheer together.

23

The two contented shall be united together,
When the most part shall be joyned to Mars,
The great one of Africa shall be in fear and terrour,
Duumuirat shall by the pursuit be disjointed.

24

The kingdom and king being raised under Venus,
Saturn shall have power over Jupiter,
The law and reign raised by Jupiter,
Through those of Saturn it will suffer the worst.

25

The Arab prince Mars, sun, Venus, leo,
The rule of the church will succumb by sea:
Towards Persia very nearly a million men,
The true serpent will invade Byzantium and Egypt.

26

The slavish people through luck in war
Be raised to so high a degree,
That they shall change their prince, and elect one among themselves,
They shall cross the sea with an army raised in the mountains.

27

By fire and sword not far from the black sea,
They shall come from Persia to seize upon Trebisonde,
Pharos and Methelin shall quake, sun be merry,
The sea of Adria shall be covered with Arabian blood.

28

The arm hanging, and the leg bound,
With a pale face, a dagger in the bosom,
Three that shall be sworn to the fray,
To the great one of Genoa the iron shall be darted.

29

The liberty shall not be recovered,
It shall be occupied, by a black, fierce, and wicked villain;
When the work of the bridge shall be ended,
The Venetian commonwealth shall be vexed.

30
All around the great city
Soldiers shall lye in the fields and towns,
Paris shall give the assault, Rome shall be attached;
Then upon the bridge shall be great plundering.

31
Through the attic land fountain of wisdom,
And now is the rose of the World,
A bridge shall be ruinated with its great preeminence,
It shall be subdued, and made a wrack by the waves.

32
Where all is good, the sun all beneficial and the moon
Is existent, his ruine draweth near,
The heaven is making hast to change thy fortune,
Into the same case as the seventh rock is

33
Of the chief men in a rebelled city,
Who shall stand out to recover their liberty,
The Males shall be cut in pieces, o unhappy quarrel!
Cries and houlings, it shall be pity to see at Nantes.

34
From the deepest part of the English West
Where the head of the British isle is
A fleet will enter the Gironde through Blois,
Through wine and salt, fires hidden in the casks.

35
For the free city of the great crescent sea,
Which still carries the stone in its stomach,
The English fleet will come under a fog
To seize a branch, war opened by the great one.

36
The bother of the sister, with a fained dissimulation,
Shall mix dew with mineral,
In a cake given to a slow old woman,
She dieth tasting of, the deed shall be simple, and country like.

37
Three hundred shall be of one mind and agreement,
That they may compass their ends,
Twenty months after by all them and their partners,
Their king shall be betrayed, by dissembling a fained hatred.

38
The great monarch that shall succeed to the great one,
Shall lead a life unlawfull, and lecherous,
By carelesness he shall give to all,
So that in the end the Salic law will fail.

39

Issued from the true branch of the fleur-de-lys,
Placed and lodged as heir of Etruria:
His ancient blood woven by long hand,
He will cause the escutcheon of Florence to bloom.

40

The royal blood shall be so much mixed,
The French shall be constrained by the Spaniards,
They shall stay till the term be past,
And the remembrance of the voice be over.

41

Being born in the shadows and nocturnal time,
He shall be a sovereign in kingdom and bounty,
He shall cause his blood to come again from the ancient urn,
Renewing a golden age instead of a brazen one.

42

Mars raised to his highest belfry
Will cause the Savoyards to withdraw from France:
The Lombard people will cause very great terror
To those of the eagle included under the Balance.

43

The great ruin of the holy things is not far off,
Provence, Naples, Sicily, Sees and Pons:
In Germany, at the Rhine and Cologne,
Vexed to death by all those of Mainz.

44

By sea the red one shall be taken by pirates,
The peace by that means shall be troubled,
He shall commit anger and coveteousness by a feigned action,
The high priest shall have a double army.

45

The great empire will soon be desolated
And transferred to near the Ardennes:
The two bastards beheaded by the oldest one,
And Bronzebeard the hawk-nose will reign.

46

By red Hats, quarrels and new schisms,
When the Sabine shall be elected,
Great sophismes shall be produced against him,
And Rome will be injured by those of Alba.

47

The great Arab will march far forward,
He will be betrayed by the Byzantinians:
Ancient Rhodes will come to meet him,
And greater harm through the Austrian Hungarians.

48

After the great affliction of the sceptre,
Two enemies will be defeated by them:
A fleet from Africa will appear before the Hungarians,
By land and sea horrible deeds will take place.

49

None out of Spain, but of the ancient France,
Shall be elected to govern the tottering ship.
The enemy shall be trusted,
Who to his kingdom shall be a cruel plague.

50

The year that the bothers of the lily come of age,
One of them will hold the great 'Romania':
The mountains to tremble, Latin passage opened,
Agreement to march against the fort of Armenia.

51

The people of Dacia, England, Poland
And of Bohemia shall make a new league,
To go beyond Hercules pillars,
The Barcelonans and Tuscans will prepare a cruel plot.

52

A king shall be, who shall be opponent
To the banished persons raised upon the kingdom,
The chast Hippolite nation shall swim in blood,
And shall flourish a great while under such an ensign.

53

The law of the sun and Venus contending,
Appropriating the spirit of prophecy,
Neither one nor the other shall be heard,
The law of the great Messiah will hold through the sun.

54

From beyond the black sea and great Tartary,
A king shall come to see France,
He shall go through Alanea and Armenia,
And shall leave a bloody rod in Constantinople.

55

In the country of Arabia Felix
There will be born one powerful in the law of Mahomet:
To vex Spain, to conquer Grenada,
And more by sea against the Ligurian people.

56

By the death of the very old high-Priest,
Shall be a Roman elected of good age,
Of whom it shall be said, that he dishonoureth the seat,
And shall live long, and be of a fierce courage.

57

There will go from Mont Gaussier and 'Aventin,'
Who through a hole shall give notice to the army,
Between two rocks the booty shall be taken,
Of Sextus' mausoleum the renown to fail.

58

By the aqueduct of Uzes over the Gard,
Through the forest and inaccessible mountain,
In the middle of the bridge there will be cut in the fist
The chief of Nimes who will be very terrible.

59

Too long a stay for the English chief at Nimes,
Towards Spain redbeard to the rescue:
Many shall die by open war that day,
When in Artois the star shall fail in the beard.

60

By a shaven head shall be made an ill choice,
That shall go beyond his commission,
He shall proceed with so great fury and rage,
That he shall put both sexes to fire and sword.

61

The child of the great man that was not at his birth,
He will subjugate the high Apennine mountains:
He will cause all those of the balance to tremble,
And from the Pyrenees to Mont Cenis.

62

It shall rain blood upon the rocks,
The sun being in the East, and Saturn in the West,
War shall be near Orgon, and great evil at Rome,
Ships shall be cast away, and the trident be taken.

63

From the vain enterprise honor and undue complaint,
Boats tossed about among the Latins, cold, hunger, waves
Not far from the Tiber the land stained with blood,
And diverse plagues will be upon mankind.

64

The gathered by the rest of the great numbers,
By land and sea shall recall their councel,
Near Autonne, Genoa, Nice in the shadow,
In fields and towns the chief shall be one against another.

65

One coming upon a suddain shall cause a great fear,
To the chief men that were hidden and concerned in the business,
And the lady Ambraise shall be seen no more,
And by little and little the great one shall be angry.

66

Under the ancient vestal edifices,
Not far from the ruined aqueduct:
The glittering metals are of the sun and moon,
The lamp of Trajan engraved with gold burning.

67

When the chief of Perugia will not venture his tunic
Sense under cover to strip himself quite naked:
Seven shall be taken for setting up aristocracy,
The Father and the son shall die by pricks in the collar.

68

In the Danube and of the Rhine will come to drink
The great camel, and shall not repent;
The Rhosne shall tremble, and more those of Loire,
And near the Alpes the cock shall ruine him.

69
The great one shall be no more in a false sleep,
The restlessness shall take rest,
He shall raise an army of gold and azure,
To subjugate Africa and gnaw it to the bone,

70
Of the regions subject to the balance,
They will trouble the mountains with great war,
Captives the entire sex enthralled and all Byzantium,
So that at dawn they will spread the news from land to land.

71
By the fury of one staying for the water,
By his great rage the whole army shall be troubled,
There shall be seventeen boats full of noblemen
The messenger come late along the Rhone.

72

By the pleasure of a voluptuous proclamation,
The poison shall be mixed in the law,
Venus shall be in so great request,
That it shall darken all the allay of the sun.

73

The church of god shall be persecuted,
And the holy temples shall be spoiled,
The child shall turn out his mother in her smock,
Arabs will be allied with the Poles.

74

Of Trojan blood will be born a Germanic heart
Who will rise to very high power:
He will drive out the foreign Arabic people,
Returning the church to its pristine pre-eminence.

75

He shall go up upon the good more on the right hand,
He shall stay sitting upon the square stone,
Towards the South; being set, on the left hand,
A crooked stick in his hand, and his mouth shut.

76

He shall pitch his Tent in the open air,
Refusing to lodge in the city,
Aix, Carpentras, Lisle, Volce, Mont Cavaillon,
In all those places, he shall abolish his trace.

77

All degrees of Ecclesiastical honor
Will be changed to that of Jupiter and Quirinus:
The priest of Quirinus to one of Mars,
Then a king of France will make him one of Vulcan.

78

The two will not be united for very long,
And in thirteen years to the Barbarian Satrap:
They shall cause such loss on both sides,
That one shall bless the boat and its covering.

79

The sacred pomp will come to lower its wings,
Through the coming of the great legislator:
He will raise the humble, he will vex the rebels,
His like will not appear on this earth.

80

Ogmios will approach great Byzantium,
The Barbaric league will be driven out:
Of the two laws the heathen one will give way,
Barbarian and Frank in perpetual strife.

81

The royal bird upon the solar city,
Seven months together shall make a nocturn augury,
The Eastern wall shall fall, the lightning shall shine,
Then the enemies shall be at the Gate for seven days.

82

At the conclusion of the treaty outside the fortress
Will not go he who is placed in despair:
When those of Arbois, of Langres against Bresse
Will have the mountains of Dole an enemy ambush.

83

Those that shall have undertaken to subvert
The kingdom that hath no equal in power and victories,
Shall cause by fraud, notice to be given for three nights together,
When the greatest shall be reading a Bible at the Table.

84

One shall be born out of the gulf and the unmeasurable city,
Born of Parents obscure and dark,
Who by the means of Rouen and Eureux,
Will go about to destroy the power of the great king.

85

Through Swedeland and the Neighbouring places,
By reason of the clouds shall fall to war,
The Lobstars, grasshoppers and gnats,
The faults of Leman shall appear very naked.

86

Divided in two heads and parted into three arms,
The great city shall be troubled with waters,
Some great ones among them scattered by banishment,
Byzantium hard pressed by the head of Persia.

87

In the year that Saturn out of slavery,
In the free country shall be drowned by water,
With Troian blood his marriage shall be,
And for certain he shall be hedged about with Spaniards.

88

Through a frightful flood upon the sand,
A marine monster from other seas found:
Near the place will be made a refuge,
Holding Savona the slave of Turin.

89

Into Hungary through Bohemia, Navarre,
And by banners fained seditions,
Through flower de Luce the country that wears the bar,
Against Orleans shall make commotions.

90

In the Cyclades, in Perinthus and Larissa,
In Sparta and the entire Pelopennesus:
Very great famine, plague through false dust,
Nine months will it last and throughout the entire peninsula.

91

At the market that they call that of liars,
Of the entire Torrent and field of Athens:
They will be surprised by the light horses,
By those of Alba when Mars is in leo and Saturn in Aquarius.

92

After the seat possessed seventeen years,
Five shall change in such a space of time;
After that, one shall be elected at the same time,
Who shall not be very conformable to the Romans.

93

Under the land of the round lunar globe,
When Mercury will be dominating:
The isle of Scotland will produce a luminary,
One who will put the English into confusion.

94

He will transfer into great Germany
Brabant and Flanders, Ghent, Bruges and Boulogne:
The truce feigned, the great duke of Armenia
Will assail Vienna and Cologne.

95

The nautical oar will tempt the shadows,
Then it will come to stir up the great empire:
In the Aegean sea the impediments of wood
Obstructing the diverted Tyrrhenian sea.

96

The rose shall be in the middle of the great world,
Blood shall be publickly spilt for new deeds;
To say the truth, every one shall stop his mouth,
Then at the time of need shall come long looked for.

97

The deformed born shall through horror be suffocated,
In the habitable city of the great king,
The severe Proclamation against banished shall be recalled,
Hail and thunder, Condom inestimable.

98

At the forty-eigth climacteric degree,
At the end of cancer very great dryness:
Fish in sea, river, lake boiled hectic,
Bearn, Bigorre in distress through fire from the sky.

99

Milan, Ferrara, Turin and Aquileia,
Capua, Brindisi vexed by the Celtic nation:
By the Lion and his eagle's phalanx,
When the old British chief Rome will have.

100

The incendiary trapped in his own fire,
Of fire from the sky at Carcassonne and the Comminges:
Foix, Auch, Mazeres, the high old man escaped,
Through those of Hesse and Thuringia, and some Saxons.

CENTURY VI

1

Around the Pyrenees mountains a great throng
Of strange nations to succour a new king;
Near Garonne and the great temple of Mas,
A Roman captain shall fear him in the water.

2

In the year five hundred fourscore more or less,
There shall be a strange age,
In the year seven hundred and three (witness heaven),
Many kingdoms, one to five shall be changed.

3

The river that tries the new Celtic heir
Will be in great discord with the empire:
The young prince through the ecclesiastical people
Will remove the sceptre of the crown of concord.

4

The Celtic river will change its course,
No longer will it include the city of Agrippina:
All changed except the old language,
Saturn, leo, Mars, cancer in plunder.

5

Very great famine through pestiferous wave,
Through long rain the length of the arctic pole:
Samarobryn a hundred leagues from the hemisphere,
Shall live without law, exempt from pollicy.

6

There will appear towards the North
Not far from cancer the bearded star:
Susa, Siena, Boeotia, Eretria,
The great one of Rome will die, the night over.

7

Norway and Dacia and the British isle
Shall be vexed by the bothers united.
The Roman captain issued from French blood,
His Forces shall be beaten back to the forest.

8

Those that were in esteem for their learning,
Upon the change of a king shall become poor,
Some banished, without help, having no gold,
Learned and learning shall not be much valued.

9

To the holy temples shall be done great scandals,
That shall be accounted for honours and praises,
By one, whose medals are graven in gold and silver,
The end of it shall be in very strange torments.

10

Within a little while the temples of the colours,
White and black shall be intermixt,
Red and Yellow shall take away their colours,
Blood, earth, plague, famine, fire, water shall destroy them.

11

The seven branches shall be reduced to three,
The eldest shall be surprised by death,
Two shall be said to kill their bothers,
The conspirators shall be killed, being asleep.

12

To raise an army, for to ascend unto the empire,
Of the Vatican, the royal blood shall endeavour,
Flemings, English, Spain shall aspire,
And shall contend against Italy and France.

13

A doubtful man shall not come far from the reign,
The greatest part will uphold him,
A capitol will not consent that he should reign,
His great chair he shall not be able to maintain.

14

Far from his land a king will lose the battle,
At once escaped, pursued, then captured,
Ignorant one taken under the golden mail,
Under false garb, and the enemy surprised.

15

Under the tomb shall be found the prince,
That shall have a price above Nuremberg,
That Spanish king in capricorn shall be thine,
Deceived and betrayed by the great Vutitemberg.

16

That which will be carried off by the young Hawk,
By the Normans of France and Picardy:
The black ones of the temple of the black forest place
Will make an inn and fire of Lombardy.

17

After the files the ass-drivers burned,
They will be obliged to change diverse garbs:
Those of Saturn burned by the millers,
Except the greater part which will not be covered.

18
The great king abandoned by the physicians,
By fate not the Jew's art he remains alive,
He and his kindred pushed high in the realm,
Pardon given to the race which denies Christ.

19
The true flame shall swallow up the lady,
That went about to burn the guiltless,
Before the assault the army shall be incouraged,
When in Seville, a monster like an ox shall be seen.

20
The feigned union shall not last long,
Some shall be changed, others for the most part reformed,
In the ships people shall be pen'd up,
Then shall Rome have a new leopard.

21
When those of the arctic pole are united together,
There shall be in the East a great fear and trembling,
One shall be newly elected, that shall bear the brunt,
Rhodes, Byzantium stained with Barbarian blood.

22
Within the land of the great heavenly temple,
Nephew murdered at London through feigned peace:
The bark will then become schismatic,
Sham liberty will be proclaimed everywhere.

23
The despight of a king, and coin being brought lower
People shall rise against their king,
Peace newly made, holy laws being made worse,
Paris was never in so severe an array.

24

Mars and the scepter, being conjoyned together,
Under cancer shall be a calamitous war,
A little while after a new king shall be anointed,
Who for a long time shall pacifie the earth.

25

By Mars contrary shall the monarchy
Of the great fisherman, be brought into ruinous trouble,
A young, black, red shall possess himself of the hierarchy,
The traitors shall undertake it on a misty day.

26

For four years the see will be held with some little good,
One libidinous in life will succeed to it:
Ravenna, Pisa and Verona will give support,
Longing to elevate the Papal cross.

27

Within the isles of five rivers to one,
Through the expansion of the great 'Chyren Selin':
Through the drizzles in the air the fury of one,
Six escaped, hidden bundles of flax.

28

The great Celt will enter Rome,
Leading with him a great number of banished men,
The great shepherd shall put to death every man,
That was united for the cock near the Alpes.

29

The holy widow hearing the news
Of her Branches put in perplexity or trouble,
That shall be skilfull in appeasing of quarrels,
By his purchase shall make a heap of shaven heads.

30

By the appearance of a feigned holiness,
The siege shall be betrayed to the enemies,
In a night that every one thought to be secure,
Near Brabant shall march those of Liege.

31

A king shall find what he so much longed for,
When a Prelate shall be censured wrongfully,
An answer to the duke will make him discontented,
Who in Milan shall put many to death.

32

By Treason one shall be beaten with rods to death,
Then the traitor shall be overcome by his disorder,
The great prisoner shall try a frivilous counsel,
When Berich shall bite anothers nose through anger.

33

His last hand bloody through Alus,
Shall not save him by sea,
Between two rivers he shall fear the military hand,
The black and Cholerick one shall make him repent.

34

The device of flying fire
Shall trouble so much the captain of the besieged,
And within shall be such mutiny,
That the besieged shall be in despair.

35

Near the bear and close to the white wool,
Aries, taurus, cancer, leo, virgo,
Mars, Jupiter, the sun will burn a great plain,
Woods and cities letters hidden in the candle.

36
Neither good nor evil through terrestrial battle
Will reach the confines of Perugia,
Pisa shall rebel, Florence shall be in an ill case,
A king being upon his Mule shall be wounded in the night time.

37
The ancient work will be finished,
Evil ruin will fall upon the great one from the roof:
Dead they will accuse an innocent one of the deed,
The guilty one hidden in the copse in the drizzle.

38
To the vanquished the enemies of peace,
After they shall have overcome Italy,
A bloody black one shall be committed,
Fire and blood shall be powerd, and water coloured with blood.

39
The child of the kingdom, through his Fathers imprisonement,
Shall be deprived of his kingdom for the delivering of his father,
Near the lake of Perugia the azure captive,
The hostage troop to become far too drunk.

40
To quench the great thirst the great one of Mainz
Will be deprived of his great dignity:
Those of Cologne will come to complain so loudly
That the great rump will be thrown into the Rhine.

41
The second head of the kingdom of Dannemark,
By those of Friezeland, and the Brittish island,
Shall cause to be spent above 100000. Mark,
Vainly endeavouring a journey into Italy.

42

To Ogmios will be left the realm
Of great Selyn, who shall do more then the rest,
Through Italy he shall spread his ensigns,
He shall govern by a prudent dissimulation.

43

For a long time will she remain uninhabited,
Around where the Seine and the Marne she comes to water:
Tried by the Thames and warriors,
The guards deceived in trusting in the repulse.

44

By night the rainbow will appear for Nantes,
By marine arts they will stir up rain:
In the gulf of Arabia a great fleet will plunge to the bottom,
In Saxony a monster will be born of a bear and a sow.

45

The governor of the kingdom being learned,
Shall not consent to the kings will:
He shall intend to set out a fleet by a contrary wind,
Which he shall put into the hands of the most disloyal.

46

A just person shall be banished,
By plague to the Borders of Non seggle,
The answer to the red one shall make him deviate,
Retiring himself to the frog and the eagle.

47

The two great ones assembled between two mountains
Will abandon their secret quarrel:
Brussels and Dole overcome by Langres,
To execute their plague at Malines.

48
The fained and seducing holiness,
Accompanied with a fluent tongue,
Shall cause the old city, and too hasty Parma,
Florence and Sienna to be more desert.

49
The great Pontiff of the party of Mars
Will subjugate the confines of the Danube:
The cross to pursue, through sword hook or crook,
Captives, gold, jewels more than one hundred thousand rubies.

50
Within the pit will be found the bones,
Incest will be commited by the stepmother:
The state changed, they will demand fame and praise,
And they will have Mars attending as their star.

51
People assembled to see a new show,
Princes and kings, with many assistants,
Pillars shall fail, walls also, but as a miracle,
The king saved, and thirty of the standers by.

52
Instead of the great one that shall be condemned
And put out of prison, his friend being in his place,
The Trojan hope in six months joyn, still born,
The sun in Aquarius, then rivers shall be frozen.

53
The great Celtic Prelate suspected by the king,
By night in flight he will leave the realm:
Through a duke fruitful for his great British king,
Byzantium to Cyprus and Tunis unsuspected.

54

At daybreak at the second crowing of the cock,
Those of Tunis, of Fez and of Bougie,
By the Arabs the king of Morocco captured,
The year sixteen hundred and seven, of the Liturgy.

55

By the appeased duke in drawing up the contract,
Arabesque sail seen, sudden discovery:
Tripolis, Chios, and those of Trebizond,
Duke captured, the black sea and the city a desert.

56

The dreaded army of the Narbonne enemy
Will frighten very greatly the 'Hesperians':
Perpignan empty through the blind one of Arbon,
Then Barcelona by sea will take up the quarrel.

57

He that was a great way in the kingdom,
Having a red head and near the hierarchy,
Harsh and cruel, shall make himself so dreadful,
That he shall succeed to the sacred monarchy.

58

Between the two monarchs that live far one from the other,
When the sun shall be eclipsed by Selene,
Great enmity shall be between them two,
So that liberty shall be restored to the isles and Sienne.

59

A lady in fury by rage of an adultery,
Shall come to her prince and conjure him to say nothing,
But shortly shall the shameful thing be known,
So that seventeen shall be put to death.

60

The prince outside his Celtic land
Will be betrayed, deceived by the interpreter:
Rouen, La Rochelle through those of Brittany
At the port of Blaye deceived by monk and priest.

61

The great carpet folded will not show
But by half the greatest part of the history,
The driven out of the kingdom shall appear sharp afar off,
In warlike matters every one shall believe him.

62

Too late both the flowers will be lost,
The serpent will not want to act against the law:
The forces of the leaguers confounded by the French,
Savona, Albenga through Monaco great martyrdom.

63
The lady shall be left to reign alone,
The only one being extinguished, first in the bed of honour,
Seven years she shall weep for grief,
After that she shall live long in the reign by good luck.

64
No agreement shall be kept,
All those that shall admit of it deal falsly,
There shall be protestations made by land and sea,
Barcelona shall take a fleet by craft.

65
Between the gray and sad gray shall be half open war,
By night they shall be assaulted and plundered,
The sad gray being taken, shall be put in custody,
His temple shall be open, two shall be put in the grate.

66
At the foundation of a new sect,
The Bones of the great Roman shall be found,
The Sepulchre shall appear covered with marble,
The earth shall quake in April, they shall be ill buried.

67
To the great empire quite another shall come,
Being farther from goodness and happiness,
Governed by one of base parentage,
The kingdom shall fall, a great unhappiness.

68
When the soldiers in a seditious fury
Will cause steel to flash by night against their chief:
The enemy Alba acts with furious hand,
Then to vex Rome and seduce the principal ones.

69
The great pity will occur before long,
Those that did give shall be constrained to receive,
Naked, famished with cold, thirst, to mutiny,
To go over the mountains making great disorders.

70
A chief of the world the great Cheiren shall be,
Moreover, beloved afterwards, feared, dreaded,
His fame and praise shall go beyond the heavens,
And shall be contented with the only title of Victor.

71
When they shall come to celebrate the obsequies of the great king,
A day before he be quite dead,
He shall be seen presently to be allyed
Through lions, eagles, cross crown sold.

72

By a faigned fury of divine inspiration,
The wife of the great one shall be ravished,
Judges willing to condemn such a doctrine,
She is sacrificed a victim to the ignorant people.

73

In a great city a monk and artisan,
Dwelling near the gate, and the walls,
Near an old woman, 'tis a secret saying cave,
A Treason shall be plotted under pretence of a marriage.

74

The expelled shall come again to the kingdom,
Her enemies shall be found to be the conspirators,
More than ever his time shall triumph,
Three and seventy appointed for death.

75

The great Pilot shall be sent for by the king,
To leave the fleet, and be preferred to a higher place,
Seven years after he shall be countermanded,
A Barbarian army shall put Venice to a fright.

76

The ancient city founded by Antenor,
Being not able to bear the tyrant any longer,
With a fained haft, in the church cut a throat,
The people will come to put his servants to death.

77

Through the fraudulent victory of the deceived,
Two fleets one, German revolt:
The chief murdered and his son in the tent,
Florence and Imola pursued into 'Romania'.

78

To proclaim the victory of the great expanding 'Selin:'
By the Romans will the eagle be demanded,
Pavia, Milan and Genoa will not consent thereto,
Then by themselves the great Lord claimed.

79

Near the Ticino the inhabitants of the Loire,
Garonne the Seine, the Tain and Gironde:
They will erect a promontory beyond the mountains,
Conflict given, Po enlarged, submerged in the wave.

80

The kingdom of Fez shall come to those of Europe,
Fire and sword shall destroy their city,
The great one of Asia by land and sea with a great troop,
So that blews, greens, crosses to death he shall drive.

81

Tears, cries and laments, howls, terror,
Heart inhuman, cruel, black and chilly:
Lake of Geneva the isles, of Genoa the notables,
Blood to pour out, wheat famine to none mercy.

82

Through the Deserts of a free and ragged place,
The Nephew of the pope shall come to wander,
Felled by seven with a heavy club,
By those who afterwards will occupy the chalice.

83

He who will have so much honor and flattery
At his entry into Belgian Gaul:
A while after shall commit so many rudenesses,
And shall be against the warlike flower.

84
He that Claudius will not have to reign in Sparta,
The same shall do so much by a deceitful way,
That he shall cause him to be arraigned short and long,
As if he had made his prospect upon the king.

85
The great city of Tarsus by the Gauls
Will be destroyed, all of the Turban captives:
Help by sea from the great one of portugal,
First day of summer urban's consecration.

86
The great Prelate the next day after his dream,
Interpreted contrary to his sense,
From Gascony shall come to him a Monge,
That shall cause the great prelate of sens to be elected.

87
The election made in Frankfort
Will be voided, Milan will be opposed:
The follower closer will seem so very strong
That he will drive him out into the marshes beyond the Rhine.

88
A great kingdom shall be left desolate,
Near the river Hebrus an assembly shall be made,
The Pyrenean mountains shall comfort him,
When in May shall be an earth-quake.

89
Between two boats one shall be tyed hand and foot,
His face annointed with Honey, and he nourished with milk,
Wasps and Bees shall make much of him in anger,
For being treacherous cup-bearers, and poisoning the cup.

90

The stinking and abominable defiling
After the secret shall succeed well,
The great one shall be excused for not being favourable,
That Neptune might be perswaded to peace.

91

The leader of the naval forces,
Red, rash, severe, horrible extortioner,
Being slave, shall escape, hidden amongst the harnesses,
When a son named Agrippa, shall be born to the great one.

92

A princess of an exquisite beauty,
Shall be brought to the general, the second time the fact shall be betrayed,
The city shall be given to the sword and fire,
By two great a murder the chief person about the king shall be hated.

93

The greedy prelate deceived by ambition,
He will come to reckong nothing too much for him:
He and his messengers completely trapped,
He who cut the wood sees all in reverse.

94

A king shall be angry against the Covenant-breakers,
When the warlike armour shall be forbidden,
The poison with sugar shall be put in the strawberries,
They shall be murdered and die, saying, close, close.

95

Calumny against the cadet by the detractor,
When enormous and Martial deeds shall be done,
The least part shall be left doubtfull to the
Eldest, and soon after they shall be both equal in the kingdom.

96
Great city abandoned to the soldiers,
There was never a mortal tumult so near,
Oh! what a hideous calamity draws near,
Except one offence nothing shall be spared.

97
The heaven shall burn at five and forty degrees,
The fire shall come near the great new city,
In an instant a great flame dispersed shall burst out,
When they shall make a trial of the Normans.

98
Ruin for the Volcae so very terrible with fear,
Their great city stained, pestilential deed:
To plunder sun and moon and to violate their temples:
And to redden the two rivers flowing with blood.

99
The learned enemy shall go back confounded,
A great camp shall be sick, and in effect through ambush,
The Pyrenean mountains shall refuse him.
Discovering near the river ancient jugs.

100
Daughter of Laura, sanctuary of the sick,
Where to the heavens is seen the amphitheatre,
A prodigy being seen, the danger is near,
Thou shalt be taken captive above four times.

CENTURY VII

1
The bow of the treasure by Achilles deceived,
Shall shew to posterity the quadrangulary,
In the royal deed the comment shall be known,
The body shall be seen hanged in the knowledge of the people.

2
Arles shall not proceed by open war,
By night the soldiers shall be astonished,
Black, white, and blew, dissembled upon the ground.
Under the fained shadow you shall see them proclaimed traitors.

3
After the naval victory of France,
The people of Barcelona the saillinons and those of Marseilles;
The robber of gold, the anvil enclosed in the ball,
Those of Toulon to the fraud shall consent.

4
The duke of Langres besieged at Dôle
Accompanied by people from Autun and Lyons.
Geneva, Augsburg allied to those of Mirandola,
To cross the mountains against the people of Ancona.

5
Wine shall be spilt upon the table,
By reason that a third man shall not have her whom he intended,
Twice the black one descended from Parma,
Shall do to Perusa and Pisa what he intended.

6
Naples, Palerma and all of Sicily
Will be uninhabited through Barbarian hands.
Corsica, Salerno and the island of Sardinia,
Hunger, plague, war the end of extended evils.

7
Upon the struggle of the great light horses,
It will be claimed that the great crescent is destroyed.
To kill by night, in the mountains,
Dressed in shepherd's' clothing, red gulfs in the deep ditch.

8
Florense, flee, flee the nearest Roman,
At Fiesole will be conflict given:
Blood shall be spilt, the greatest shall be taken,
Temple nor sex shall be spared.

9
A lady in the absence of her great captain,
Shall be intreated of love by the Viceroy,
A fained promise, and unhappy new years gift,
In the hand of the great prince of Bar.

10
By the great prince bordering Le Mans,
brave and valiant leader of the great army;
by land and sea with Bretons and Normans,
To pass Gibraltar and Barcelona to pillage the island.

11
The royal child shall despise his mother,
Eye, feet wounded, rude disobedient,
News to a lady very strange and bitter,
There shall be killed of hers above five hundred.

12
The great younger bother shall make an end of the war,
In two places he shall gather the excused,
Cahors and Moissac will go far from the prison,
A refusal at Lectoure, the people of agen shaved.

13
Of the city maritine and tributary,
The shaven head shall take the government,
He shall turn out a base man who shall be against him,
During fourteen years he will keep the tyranny.

14
They shall expound topography falsly,
The urnes of the monuments shall be open,
Sects shall multiply, and holy philosophy
Shall give black for white, and green for old.

15
Before a city of Piemont,
Seven years the siege shall be laid,
The most great king shall make his entry into it,
Then the city shall be free being out of the enemies hand.

16
The deep entry made by the queen,
Shall make the place powerful and inaccessible,
The army of the three lions shall be routed,
Doing within an hideous and terrible thing.

17
The prince who has little pity of mercy
After he shall have given peace to his subjects,
Shall by death change his great knowledge,
After great rest the kingdom shall be troubled.

18
The besieged will color their pacts,
Seven days after they shall make a cruel event,
They shall be beaten back, fire, blood, seven put to death,
The lady shall be prisoner who endeavoured to make peace.

19
The fort at Nice will not engage in combat,
By shining metal it shall be overcome,
The doing of it shall be long and debating,
It shall be a strange fearful thing to the citizens.

20
Ambassadors of the Tuscan language
Will cross the Alps and the sea in April and May.
One like a calf shall make a speech:
Attempting to defame the French customes.

21
By a pestilent Italian enmity,
The dissembler shall expel thetyrant,
The bargain shall be made at Sorgues bridge,
To put him and his adherent to death.

22
The citizens of Mesopotamia
Angry with their friends from Tarraconne;
games, rites, banquets, every person asleep,
The vicar at Rhône, the city taken and those of Ausonia.

23
The royal scepter shall be constrained to take
What his Predecessors had morgaged;
After that, they shall mis-inform the Lamb,
When they shall come to plunder the palace.

24
The buried shall come out of his grave,
He shall cause the fort of the bridge to be tied with chains,
Poisoned with the spawn of a pimp,
Shall a great one of Lorrain be by the Marques du pont.

25
By a long war, all the army drained dry,
So that to raise soldiers they shall find no money,
Instead of gold and silver, they shall stamp leather,
The French copper, the mark of the stamp the new moon.

26
Fly-boats and Galleys round about seven ships,
A mortal war there shall be,
The chief of Madrid shall receive blows of oars,
Two shall escape, and five carried to land.

27
At the wall of Vasto the great cavalry
Are impeded by the baggage near Ferrara.
At Turin they will speedily commit such robbery
That in the fort they will ravish their hostage.

28
The captain shall lead a great prey
Upon the mountain, that shall be nearest to the enemies,
Being encompassed with fire, he shall make such a way,
That all shall escape, but thirty that shall be spitted.

29
The great duke of Alba shall rebel,
To his Grandfathers he shall make the plot,
The great man of Guise will come to vanquish him,
Led prisoner, and a monument erected.

30
The sack approaches, fire and great bloodshed.
Po the great rivers, the enterprise for the clowns;
After a long wait from Genoa and Nice,
Fossano, Turin the capture at Savigliano.

31
From Languedoc and Guienne more than ten
Thousand will want to cross the Alps again.
The great Savoyards march against Brindisi,
Aquino and Bresse will come to drive them back.

32
Out of the royal mount shall be born in a cottage,
One that shall tyranise over duke and earl,
He shall raise an army in the land of Millan,
To drain Faenza and Florence of gold and men.

33
By fraud a kingdom and an army shall be spoilt,
The fleet shall be put to a strait, passages shall be made to the spies,
Two feigned friends shall agree together,
They shall raise up a hatred that had been long dormant.

34
In great regret shall the French nation be.
Their vain and light heart shall believe rashly.
They shall have neither bread, salt, wine, nor beer,
Moreover they shall be prisoners, and shall suffer hunger, cold, and need.

35
The great Pocket shall bewaile and bemoan,
For having elected one, they shall be deceived in his age,
He shall not stay long with them,
He shall be deceived by those of his own language.

36

God, the heavens, all the divine words in the waves,
carried by seven red-shaven heads to Byzantium:
Against the anointed three hundred from Trebizond,
Will make two laws, first horror then trust.

37

Ten sent to put the captain of the ship to death,
Are altered by one that there is open revolt in the fleet.
Confusion, the leader and another stab and bite each other
At Lerins and the Hyerès, ships, prow into the darkness.

38

The eldest royal prancing upon a horse,
Shall spur, and run very fiercely
Open mouth, the foot in the stirrup, complaining,
Drawn, pulled, die horribly.

39

The leader of the French army
Will expect to lose the main phalanx.
Upon the pavement of oats and slate
The foreign nation will be undermined through Genoa.

40

Within casks anointed outside with oil and grease
Before the harbour, one and twenty shall be shut,
At the second watch, by death, they shall do great feats of arms,
To win the gates, and be killed by the watch.

41

The bones of the feet and of the hands in shackles,
By a noise a house shall be a long time deserted,
By a dream the buried shall be taken out of the ground,
The house shall be healthful, and inhabited without noise.

42

Two newly come being provided with poison,
To pour in the kitchen of the great prince,
By the cooks boy the fact shall be known,
And he taken, that thought by death to vex the elder.

CENTURY VIII

1

Pau, Nay, Loron will be more of fire than blood,
To swim in praise, the great one to flee to the confluence (of rivers).
He will refuse entry to the magpies,
Pampon, Durance shall keep them enclosed.

2

Condon and Aux, and about Mirande,
I see a fire from heaven that encompasseth them,
Sol, Mars, in conjunction with the lion, and then Marmande,
Lightning, great war, wall falls into the Garonne.

3

In the strong castle of Vigilanne and Resviers,
Shall be kept close the youngest son of Nancy,
Within Turin the first shall be burnt up,
When Lyon shall be overwhelmed with sorrow.

4

The cock will be received into Monace,
The cardinal of France will appear;
He will be deceived by the Roman legation;
Weakness to the eagle, strength will be born to the cock.

5

A shining adorned temple shall appear,
The Lamp and wax candle at Borne and Bretueil,
For Lucerne the Canton turned of,
When the great cock shall be seen in his coffin.

6

A thundering light at Lyons appearing,
Bright, took Malta, instantly shall be put out,
Sardon shall treat Mauris deceitfully,
To Geneva, London, and the cock a fained treason.

7

Vercelli, Milan will give the news,
The wound will be given at Pavia.
Run through Seine water, blood, fire through Florence,
The only one shall fall from top to bottom making maye.

8

Near Focia enclosed in some tuns
Chivasso will plot for the eagle.
The elect cashiered, he and his men shut up,
Within Turin, a rape, and bride carried away.

9

While the eagle is united with the cock at Savonna,
The Eastern sea and Hungary.
The army at Naples, Palermo, the marches of Ancona,
Rome and Venice a great outcry by the Barbarian.

10

A great stench will come from Lausanne,
but they will not know its origin,
They will put out all people from distant places,
Fire seen in the sky, a foreign nation defeated.

11

A multitude of people will appear at Vicenza
Without force, fire to burn the Basilica.
Near Lunage the great one of Valenza defeated:
At a time when Venice takes up the quarrel through custom.

12
He will appear near to Buffalora
The highly born and tall one entered into Milan.
The Abbe of Foix with those of Saint-Meur
Will cause damage dressed up as serfs.

13
The crusader bother through impassioned love
Will cause bellerophon to die through Proteus;
Fleet to thousand years, the woman out of her wit,
The drink being drunk, both after that, perish.

14
The great credit, the abundance of gold and silver
Shall blind honour by lust,
The offence of the adulterer shall be known,
Which shall come to his great dishonour.

15
Towards the North great endeavours by a manly woman,
To trouble Europe, and almost all the world,
She shall put to flight the two eclipses,
That they will reinforce life or death for the Hungarians.

16
In the place where Jason caused his ship to be built,
So great a Flood shall be, and so sudden,
That there shall be neither place nor land to save themselves,
The waves shall climb upon the Olympic Fesulan.

17
Those that were at ease shall be put down,
The world shall be put in trouble by three bothers,
The maritine city shall be seized by its enemies,
Hunger, fire, blood, plague, and the double of all evils.

18

The cause of her death will be issued from Florence,
One time before, through fasting and old drink,
For the three Lillies shall make her such a pause,
Saved by her fruit, as raw flesh dead.

19

To maintain up the great troubled cloak,
The red ones shall march for to clear it,
A family shall be almost crushed to death,
The red, the red, shall knock down the red one.

20

The false message about the rigged election
To run through the city stopping the broken pact;
Voices shall be bought, and a chapel died with blood,
By another, who challengeth the empire.

21

Three galleys shall come into the harbour of Agde,
Carrying with them infection and pestilence,
Going beyond the bridge, they shall carry away thousands,
At the third resistance the bridge shall be broken.

22

Coursan, Narbonne through the salt to warn
Tuchan, the grace of Perpignan betrayed;
The red town will not wish to consent to it,
In a high flight, a copy flag and a life ended.

23

Letters found in the queens coffers,
No superscription, no name of the author,
By policy shall be concealed the offers,
So that no body shall know who shall be the lover.

24
The Lieutenant shall at the doors entry.
Knock down the great one of Perpignan:
Thinking to save himself at Montpertuis,
The bastard of Lusignan will be deceived.

25
The Lovers heart being by a stoln love,
Shall cause the dame to be ravished in the brook,
The lascivious shall counterfeit half a discontent,
The Father shall deprive the bodies of both of their souls.

26
The Carones fond in Barcelona,
Put discovered, place soil and ruine,
The great that hold will not Pampelona,
Wants Pamplona, drizzle at the abbey of Montserrat.

27
The auxiliary way, one arch upon the other,
Being brave and gallant put out of the iron vessel,
The writing of the emperor the Phoenix,
In it shall be seen, what no where else is.

28
The copies of gold and silver inflated,
Which after the theft were thrown into the lake,
At the discovery that all is exhausted and dissipated by the debt.
All scrips and bonds will be wiped out.

29
At the fourth Pillar where they sacrifice to Saturn,
Cloven by an earth-quake and a flood,
An urne shall be found under that Saturnian building,
Full of Capion gold stoln, and then restored.

30

In Toulouse, not far from Beluzer
Digging a well, for the palace of spectacle,
A treasure found that shall vex every one,
In two parcels, in, and near the Basacle.

31

The first great fruit of the prince of Perchiera,
But he shall become very cruel and malicious,
He shall loose his fierce pride in Venice,
And shall be put to evil by the younger Celin.

32

French king, beware of your nephew
Who shall cause that thine only son
Shall be murdered making a vow to Venus,
Accompanied with three and six.

33

The great one of Verona and Vicenza shall be born,
Who shall bear a very unworthy surname,
Who shall endeavour at Venice to avenge himself,
But he shall be taken by a watch-man.

34

After the victory of the lion over the lion,
There will be great slaughter on the mountain of Jura;
Floods and dark-colored people of the seventh of a million,
Lyons, Ulm at the mausoleum death and the tomb.

35

At the entrance to Garonne and Baise
And the forest not far from Damazan,
Discoveries of the frozen sea, then hail and north winds.
Frost in the Dardonnais through the mistake of the month.

36

It will be committed against the anointed brought
From Lons le Saulnier, Saint Aubin and bell'oeuvre.
To pave with marble taken from distant towers,
Not to resist Bletteram and his masterpiece.

37

The strong fort near the Thames
Shall fall then, the king that was kept within,
Shall be seen near the bridge in his shirt,
One dead before, then in the fort kept close.

38

The king of Blois in Avignon shall reign
Another time the people do murmur,
He shall cause in the Rhosne to be bathed through the walls,
As many as five, the last shall be near Nolle.

39

He who will have been for the Byzantine prince
Will be taken away by the prince of Toulouse.
The faith of Foix through the leader of Tolentino
Will fail him, not refusing the bride.

40

The blood of the Just for Taur and La Duarade
In order to avenge itself against the Saturnines.
They will immerse the band in the new lake,
Then they will march against Alba.

41

A Fox shall be elected that said nothing,
Making a publick saint, living with barley bread,
Shall tyrannise after upon a sudden,
And put his foot upon the throat of the greatest.

42

Through avarice, through force and violence
The chief of Orléans will come to vex his supporters.
Near St. Memire, assault and resistance.
Dead in his tent they will say he is asleep inside.

43

Through the fall of two bastard creatures
The nephew of the blood will occupy the throne.
Within Lectoure there will be blows of lances,
The nephew through fear will fold up his standard.

44

The natural begotten of Ogmyon,
From seven to nine shall put out of the way,
To king of long, and friend to the half man,
Ought to Navarre prostrate the fort of Pau

45

With his hand in a sling and his leg bandaged,
The younger bother of Calais will reach far.
At the watch word his death shall be protracted,
Then afterwards at easter he shall bleed in the temple.

46

Paul the celibate will die three leagues from Rome,
The two nearest flee the oppressed monster.
For Mars shall keep such a horrible throsne,
Of cock and eagle, of France three bothers.

47

Lake Trasimene will bear witness
Of the conspirators locked up inside Perugia.
A fool will imitate the wise one,
Killing the Teutons, destroying and cutting to pieces.

48.
Saturn in cancer, Jupiter with Mars,
In February Caldondon, Salvaterre,
Sault, Castalon, assaulted on three sides,
Near Verbiesque, fight and mortal war.

49
Satur in Ox, Jupiter in water, Mars in arrow,
The sixth of February shall give mortality,
Those of Tardaigne shall make in Bruges so great a breach,
That the chief Barbarin shall die at Pontrose.

50
The plague around Capellades,
Another famine is near to Sagunto.
The Knight bastard of the good old man,
Shall cause the great one of Tunis to be beheaded.

51
The Byzantine makes an oblation
After having taken back Cordoba.
His way long, rest, contemplation,
Crossing the sea hath taken a prey by Cologne.

52
The king of Blois shall reign in Avignon,
He shall come from Amboise and Seme, along the Linder,
A Nail at Poitiers shall ruine the holy wings,
Before Bony.

53
Within Boulogne he will want to wash away his misdeeds,
In the church of the sun, but he shall not be able,
He shall fly doing so high things,
That the like was never in hierarchy.

54

Under pretence of a treaty of marriage,
A Magnanimous act shall be done by the great Cheiren Selin,
Quintin, Arras recovered in the journey,
By the Spanish a second butcher's bench is made.

55

Between two rivers he shall find himself shut up,
Tuns and barrels put together to pass over,
Eight bridges broken, the chief at last in prison,
Compleat children shall have their throat cut.

56

The weak party shall occupy the ground,
Those of the high places shall make fearful cries,
It shall trouble the great flock in the right corner,
Near Edinburgh it falls discovered by the writings.

57

From a simple soldier he shall come to have the supreme command,
From a short gown he shall come to the long one,
Vaillant in Arms, no worse man in the church,
He vexes the priests as water fills a sponge.

58

A kingdom in dispute, and divided between the bothers,
To take the arms and the name of Britain.
And the English title, he shall advise himself late,
Surprised in the night and carried into the French air.

59

Twice set up high, and twice brought down,
The East also the West shall weaken,
His adversary after many fights,
Expelled by sea, shall fail in need.

60

The first in France, the first in Romania,
By sea and land to the English and Paris,
Wonderful deeds by that great company,
Violent, the wild beast will lose Lorraine.

61

Never by the discovering of the day,
He shall attain to the sceptriferous sign,
Till all his seats be settled,
Bringing to the cock the gift of the armed legion.

62

When one sees the holy temple plundered,
The greatest of the Rhône profaning their sacred things;
From them shall come so great a pestilence,
That the king being unjust shall not condemn them.

63

When the Adulterer wounded without a blow,
Shall have murdered the wife and son by spight,
The woman knocked down, shall strangle the child,
Eight taken prisoners, and stifled without tarrying.

64

In the islands the children shall be transported,
The two of seven shall be in despair,
Those of the country shall be supported by,
Nompelle taken, avoid the hope of the league.

65

The old man frustrated of his chief hope,
He shall attain to the head of his empire,
Twenty months he shall keep the kingdom with great power,
Tyrant, cruel, and having a worse one.

66

When the writing D. M. shall be found,
And an ancient cave discovered with a lamp,
Law, king, and prince Ulpian tried,
The queen and duke in the pavilion under cover.

67

Paris, Carcassone, France to ruin in great disharmony,
Neither one nor the other will be elected.
France will have the love and good will of the people,
Ferara, Colonna great protection.

68

An old Cardinal shall be cheated by a young one,
And shall see himself out of his imployment,
Arles do not show, a double fort perceived,
And the aqueduct, and the embalmed prince.

69

Near the young one the old angel shall bowe,
And shall at last overcome him,
Ten years equal, to make the old one stoop,
Of three, two, one, the eighth a seraphin.

70

He will enter, wicked, unpleasant, infamous,
Tyrannizing over Mesopotamia.
All friends made by the adulterous lady,
The land dreadful and black of aspect.

71

The number of Astronomers shall grow so great,
Driven away, bannished, books censured,
The year one thousand six hundred and seven by sacred glomes,
That none shall be secure in the sacred places.

72

Oh what a huge defeat on the Perugian battlefield
And the fight about Ravenna,
Sacred passage when the feast shall be celebrated,
The victorious vanquished, the horse to eat up his oats.

73

A Barbarous soldier shall strike the king,
Unjustly, not far from death,
The covetous mother shall be the cause of it,
The Conspirator and kingdom in great remorse.

74

A king entered very far into the new land
Whilst his Subjects shall come to welcom him,
His perfidiousness shall find such an encounter,
That to the citizens it shall be instead of feast and welcome.

75

The father and son will be murdered together,
The leader within his pavilion.
The mother at Tours will have her belly swollen with a son,
A verdure chest with little pieces of paper.

76

More of a butcher than a king in England,
Born in obscure place, by force shall reign,
Of loose disposition, without faith, without law, the ground shall bleed,
His time is drawing so near that I sigh for it.

77

By Antichrist three shall shortly be brought to nothing,
His war shall last seven and twenty years,
The Hereticks dead, prisoners banished,
Blood, humane body, water made red, earth hailed.

78

A soldier of fortune with twisted tongue
Will come to the sanctuary of the gods.
He will open the door to heretics
And raise up the church militant.

79

He who loses his father by the sword, born in a nunnery,
Upon this gorgon's blood will conceive anew;
In a strange land he will do everything to be silent,
He who will burn both himself and his child.

80

The blood of the innocent widow and virgin,
So many evils committed by the means of that great rogue,
Holy Images, dipt in burning wax candles,
For fear no body shall be seen to stir.

81

The new empire in desolation,
Shall be changed from the Northern pole,
The commotion shall come from Sicily,
To trouble the undertaking, tributary to Philip.

82

Long gnawer, dry, cringing and fawning,
In conclusion shall have nothing but leave to be gone,
Piercing poison and letters in his collar,
Shall be seised, escape, and in danger.

83

The largest sail set out of the port of Zara,
Near Byzantium will carry out its enterprise.
There shall be no loss of foes or friends,
The third shall make a great pillage upon the two

84

Paterno will hear the cry from Sicily,
All the preparations in the gulf of Trieste;
It will be heard as far as Sicily
Flee oh, flee, so may sails, the dreaded pestilence!

85

Between Bayonne and St. Jean de Luz
Will be placed the promontory of Mars.
To the Hanix of the North, Nanar will remove the light,
Then suffocate in bed without assistance.

86

Through Emani, Tolosa and Villefranche,
An infinite band through the mountains of Adrian.
Passes the river, Cambat over the plank for a bridge,
Bayonne will be entered all crying Bigoree.

87

A conspired death shall come to an effect,
Charge given, and a journey of death,
Elected, created, received, by his own defeated,
Blood of Innocency before him by remorse.

88

A noble king shall come into Sardinia,
Who shall hold the kingdom only three years,
He shall joyn many colours to his own,
Himself afterwards, care, sleep matrirscome.

89

That he might not fall into the hands of his uncle,
That had murdered his children for to rule,
Taking away from the people, and putting his foot upon Peloncle,
Dead and drawn among armed horses.

90

When those of the cross are found their senses troubled,
In place of sacred things he will see a horned bull,
Through the virgin the pig's place will then be filled,
Order will no longer be maintained by the king.

91

Entered among the field of the Rhône
Where those of the cross are almost united,
The two lands meeting in Pisces
And a great number punished by the flood.

92

Far distant from his kingdom, sent on a dangerous journey,
He shall lead a great army, which he shall make his own,
The king shall keep his prisoners, and pledges,
At his return he shall plunder all the country.

93

For seven months, no longer, will he hold the office of prelate,
Through his death a great schism will arise;
For seven months another acts as prelate near Venice,
peace and union are reborn.

94

In front of the lake where the dearest one was destroyed
For seven months and his army routed;
Spaniards will be devastating by means of Alba,
Through delay in giving battle, loss.

95

The Deceiver shall be put into the dungeon,
And bound fast for a while,
The scholar joins the chief with his cross.
Pricking upright, shall draw in the contented.

96

The synagogue barren, without fruit,
Shall be received among the Infidels,
In Babylon, the daughter of the persecuted,
Miserable and sad shall cut her wings.

97

At the end of the Var the great powers change;
Near the bank three beautiful children are born.
Ruin to the people when they are of age;
In the country the kingdom is seen to grow and change more.

98

The blood of churchmen shall be spilt,
As water in such abundance,
And for a good while shall not be stayed,
Ruine and grievance shall be seen to the clerk.

99

By the power of three Temporal kings,
The holy See shall be put in another place,
Where the substance of the corporeal spirit,
Shall be restored and admitted for a true seat.

100

Through the abundance of the army scattered,
High and low, low and high,
Too great a belief a life lost in jesting,
To die by thirst, through abundance of want.

CENTURY IX

1

In the house of the translator of Boure,
The Letters shall be found upon the table,
Blind of one eye, red, white, hoary, shall keep its course,
Which shall change at the coming of the new constable.

2

From the top of mount Aventin, a voice was heard,
Get you gone, get you gone on all sides.
The anger will be appeased by the blood of the red ones,
From Rimini and Prato, the Colonna expelled.

3

The "great cow" at Racenna in great trouble,
Led by fifteen shut up at Fornase:
At Rome shall be born two monsters with a double head,
Blood, fire, Flood, the greater ones astonished.

4

The year following being discovered by a flood,
Two chiefs elected, the first shall not hold,
To fly from shade, to one shall be a refuge,
That house shall be plundered which shall maintain the first.

5

The third toe of the foot shall be like the first,
To a new high monarch come from low estate,
He who will possess himself as a tyrant of Pisa and Lucca,
To correct the fault of his predecessor.

6

An infinity of Englishmen in Guienne
Will settle under the name of Anglaquitaine:
In Languedoc, Ispalme, Bordelais,
Which they will name after Barboxitaine.

7

He that shall open the tomb found,
And shall not close it up again presently,
Evil will befall him, and he shall not be able to prove
Whether is best a Britain or Norman king.

8

A younger king causeth his father to be put
To a dishonest death, after a battle,
Writing shall be found, that shall give suspicion and remorse,
When a hunted wolf shall rest upon a truckle bed.

9

When a Lamp burning with unquenchable fire,
Shall be found in the temple of the Vestals,
A child shall be found, water running through a sieve,
To perish in water Nîmes, Toulouse the markets to fall.

10

The child of a monk and nun exposed to death,
To die through a she-bear, and carried off by a boar,
The army will be camped by Foix and Pamiers,
Against Toulouse Carcassonne the harbinger to form.

11

Wrongly will they come to put the just one to death,
In public and in the middle extinguished:
So great a plague shall break into that place,
That the Judges shall be compelled to run away.

12

The so much silver of Diana and Mercury,
The statues shall be found in the lake,
The Potter seeking for new clay,
He and his shall be filled with gold.

13

The banished about sologne,
Being conducted by night to go into Auxois,
Two of Modena for Bologna cruel,
Placed discovered by the fire of Buzanais.

14

A Dyers kettle being put an a plein,
With wine, honey and oil, and built upon furnace,
Shall be dipt, without evil, called malefactors,
Seven of Bordeaux smoke still in the cannon.

15
Near Perpignan the red ones detained,
Those of the middle completely ruined led far off:
Three cut in pieces, and five badly supported,
For the Lord and Prelate of Burgundy.

16
Out of Castel Franco shall come the assembly,
The Embassador not pleased, shall make a schisme,
Those of Riviere shall be in the medley,
And shall deny the entry of the great gulf.

17
The third first, worse than ever did Nero,
Go out valliant, he shall spill much humane blood,
He shall cause the Forneron to be builded again,
Golden age dead, new king great troubles.

18

The lily of the Dauphin will reach into Nancy,
As far as Flanders the elector of the empire:
New confinement for the great Montmorency,
Outside proven places delivered to celebrated punishment.

19

In the middle of the forest of Mayenne,
Sol being in leo the lightning shall fall,
The great bastard begot by the great du Main,
That day Fougeres shall enter its point into blood.

20

By night will come through the forest of Reines,
Two couples roundabout route queen the white stone,
The monk king in gray in Varennes:
Elected Capet causes tempest, fire, blood, slice.

21

At the tall temple of Saint-Solenne at Blois,
Night Loire bridge, prelate, king killing outright:
Crushing victory in the marshes of the pond,
Whence prelacy of whites miscarrying.

22

The king and his court in the place of cunning tongue,
Within the temple facing the palace:
In the garden the duke of Mantua and Alba,
Alba and Mantua dagger tongue and palace.

23

The youngest son playing under the tun,
The top of the house shall fall upon his head,
The father king in the temple of Saint-Solonne,
Sacrificing he will consecrate festival smoke.

24
Upon the palace at the balcony of the windows,
The two little royal ones will be carried off:
To pass Orléans, Paris, abbey of Saint-Denis,
Nun, wicked ones to swallow green pits.

25
Crossing the bridges to come near the Roisiers,
Sooner than he thought, he arrived late.
The new Spaniards will come to Béziers,
So that this chase will break the enterprise.

26
Departed by the bitter letters the surname of Nice,
The great Cappe will present something, not his own;
Near Voltai at the wall of the green columns,
After Piombino the wind in good earnest.

27
The Fence being of wood, close wind, bridge shall be broken,
He that's received high, shall strike at the dolphin,
The old Teccon shall pass over smooth wood,
Going over the right confines of the duke.

28
The Allied fleet from the port of Marseilles,
In Venice harbor to march against Hungary.
To leave from the gulf and the bay of Illyria,
Devastation in Sicily, for the Ligurians, cannon shot.

29
When he that giveth place to no body,
Shall forsake the place taken, and not taken,
Fire, ship, by bleeding bituminous at Charlieu,
Then Quintin and Bales shall be taken again.

30

At the port of Pola and of San Nicolo,
A Normand will punish in the gulf of Quarnero:
Capet to cry alas in the streets of Byzantium,
Help from Cadiz and the great Philip.

31

The trembling of the earth at Mortara
The tin island of St. George half sunk;
The war shall awake the sleeping pace,
Upon Easterday shall be a great hole sunk in the church.

32

A deep column of fine porphyry is found,
Under whose basis shall be Roman writings,
Bones, haires twisted, Roman force tried,
A fleet a gathering about the port of Methelin.

33

Hercules king of Rome and of "Annemark,"
With the surname of the chief of triple Gaul,
Italy and the one of St. Mark to tremble,
First monarch renowned above all.

34

The single part afflicted will be mitered,
Return conflict to pass over the tile:
For five hundred one to betray will be titled
Narbonne and Salces we have oil for knives.

35

And fair Ferdinand will be detached,
Shall leave the flower to follow the Macedonian,
At his great need his way shall fail him,
And he shall go against the Myrmidon.

36

A great king taken in the hands of a young one,
Not far from easter, confusion, stroke of a knife,
Shall commit, pittiful time, the fire at the top of the mast,
Three bothers then shall wound one another, and murder done.

37

Bridge and mills overturned in December,
The Garonne will rise to a very high place:
Walls, edifices, Toulouse overturned,
So that none will know his place like a matron.

38

The entry at Blaye for La Rochelle and the English,
The great Macedonian will pass beyond:
Not far from agen shall expect the French,
Help from Narbonne deceived by entertainment.

39

In Albisola to Veront and Carcara,
Led by night to seize Savona:
The quick Gascon La Turbie and L'Escarène:
Behind the wall old and new palace to seize.

40

Near Saint-Quintin in the forest deceived,
In the Abbey the Flemish will be cut up:
The two younger sons half a stonished with blows,
The followers oppressed, and the guards all cut in pieces.

41

The great Cheyren shall seize upon Avignon,
Letters from Rome shall come full of bitterness,
Letters and embassies shall go from Chanignon,
Carpentras taken by a black duke with a red feather.

42

From Barcelona, from Genoa and Venice,
From Sicily near Manaco united,
Against the Barbarian the fleet shall take her aim,
The Barbarian shall be driven back as far as Tunis.

43

On the point of landing the crusader army
Will be ambushed by the Ishmaelites,
Being beaten on all sides by the ship Raviere,
Presently assaulted by ten chosen galleys.

44

Go forth, go forth out of Geneva all,
Saturn of gold, shall be changed into iron,
They against Raypos shall extermine them all,
Before it happeneth, the heavens will shew signs.

45

None will remain to ask,
Great Mendosus will obtain his dominion:
Far from the court he will cause to be countermanded
Piedmont, Picardy, Paris, Tuscany the worst.

46

Get you gone, run away from Thoulouse ye red ones,
There shall expiation be made of the sacrifice,
The chief cause of the evil under the shade of gourdes,
Shall be strangled, a presage of the destruction of much flesh.

47

The underwritten to an unworthy deliverance,
Shall have from the multitude a contrary advice,
They shall change their monarch and put him in peril,
They shall see themselves shut up in a cage over against.

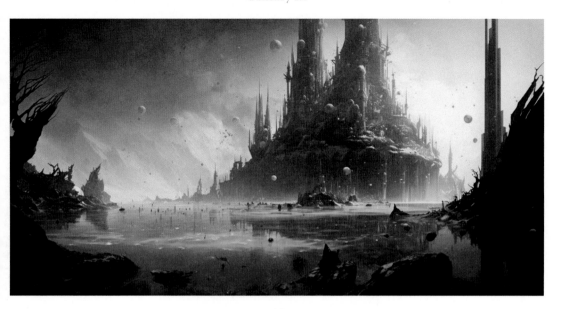

48

The great maritime city of the ocean,
Encompassed with chrystaline fens,
In the winter solstice and in the spring,
Shall be tempted with fearful wind.

49

Ghent and Brussels will march against Antwerp,
The senat of London shall put their king to death,
The salt and wine shall not be able to do him good,
That they may have the kingdom into ruine.

50

Mendosus will soon come to his high realm,
Putting behind a little the Lorrainers:
The pale red one, the male in the interregnum,
The fearful youth and Barbaric terror.

51

Against the red, Sects shall gather themselves,
Fire, water, iron, rope, by peace it shall de destroyed,
Those that shall conspire shall not be put to death,
Except one, who above all shall undo the world.

52

Peace is coming on one side and war on the other,
There was never so great a pursuing,
Man, Woman shall bemoan, innocent blood shall be spilt,
It shall be in France on all sides.

53

The young Nero in the three chimneys.
Shall cause pages to be thrown to be burnt alive,
Happy shall he be who shall be far from this doing,
Three of his own blood shall cause him to be put to death.

54
There will arrive at porto Corsini,
Near Ravenna, those that shall plunder the lady,
In the deep sea shall be the embassador of Lisbonne,
The hidden under the rock, shall carry away seventy souls.

55
The horrible war which is being prepared in the West,
The following year will come the pestilence
So very horrible that young, old, nor beast,
Blood, fire Mercury, Mars, Jupiter in France.

56
The army near Houdan will pass Goussainville,
And at Maiotes it will leave its mark:
In an instant more than a thousand will be converted,
Looking for the two to put them back in chain and firewood.

57

In the place of Drux a king shall rest himself,
And shall seek law changing Anatheme,
In the mean while the heaven shall thunder so strongly,
That a new gate shall kill the king him self.

58

On the left hand over against Vitry,
The three red ones of France shall be watched for,
All the red shall be knockt dead, the black not murdered,
By the Britains set up again in security.

59

At La Ferté-Vidame he will seize,
Nicholas held red who had produced his life:
The great Louise who will act secretly one will be born,
Giving Burgundy to the Bretons through envy.

60

A Barbarian fight in the black corner,
Blood shall be spilt, Dalmatia shall tremble for fear,
Great Ismael shall set up his promontory,
Frogs shall tremble, portugal shall bring succour.

61

The plunder made upon the marine coast,
In Cittanova and relatives brought forward:
Several of Malta through the deed of Messina
Will be closely confined poorly rewarded.

62

To the great one of Ceramon-agora,
The crusaders will all be attached by rank,
The long-lasting Opium and Mandrake,
The Raugon will be released on the third of October.

63

Complaints and tears, cries, and great howlings,
Near Narbonne, Bayonne and in Foix,
O what horrid calamities and changes,
Before Mars hath made sometimes his revolution.

64

The Macedonian to pass the Pyrenees mountains,
In March Narbon shall make no resistance,
By sea and land he shall make so much ado,
Cap. shall not have safe ground to live in.

65

He shall come into the corner of Luna,
Where he shall be taken and put in a strange land,
The green fruits shall be in great disorder,
A great shame, to one shall be great praise.

66

Peace, union, shall be, and mutation,
States, and offices, low high, and high low,
A journey shall be prepared for, the first fruit, pains,
War shall cease, as also, civil suits, and strifes.

67

From the height of the mountains around the Isère,
One hundred assembled at the haven in the rock Valence:
From Châteauneuf, Pierrelatte, in Donzère,
Against Crest, Romans, faith assembled.

68

From mount Aymar shall proceed a noble obscurity,
The evil shall come to the joyning of the Saone and Rhosne,
Soldiers shall be hid in the wood on St. Lucy's day,
So that there was never such an horrid throne.

69

One the mountain of Saint-Bel and L'Arbresle
Shall be hidden the fierce ones of Grenoble,
Beyond Lyons, Vienna, upon them shall fall such a hail,
That languishing upon the ground, the third part shall not be left.

70

Sharp weapons shall be hidden in burning torches,
In Lyons the day of the sacrament,
Those of Vienna shall be all cut to pieces,
By the latin cantons Mâcon does not lie.

71

At the holy places animals seen with hair,
With him that shall not dare in the day,
In Carcassonne for a favourable disgrace,
He shall be set to make a longer stay.

72
Again will the holy temples be polluted,
And plundered by the senate of Toulouse:
Saturn two three cycles completed,
In April, May, people of new leaven.

73
The blue Turban king entered into Foix,
And he will reign less than an evolution of Saturn:
The white turban king Byzantium heart banished,
Sun, Mars and Mercury near aquarius.

74
In the city of Fertsod homicide,
Deed, and deed many oxen plowing no sacrifice:
Return again to the honors of Artemis,
And to Vulcan bodies dead ones to bury.

75
From Ambracia and the country of Thrace
People by sea, evil and help from the Gauls:
In Provence the perpetual trace,
With vestiges of their custom and laws.

76
With the rapacious and blood-thirsty king,
Issued from the pallet of the inhuman Nero:
Between two rivers military hand left,
He will be murdered by young baldy.

77
The kingdom being taken, the king shall invite,
The lady taken to death,
The life shall be denied unto the queens son,
And the Pellix shall be at the height of the consort.

78
The Greek lady of exquisite beauty,
Made happy by countless suitors:
Transferred out to the Spanish realm,
Shall be made a prisoner, and die a miserable death.

79
The commander of a fleet by fraud and stratagem,
Shall cause the fearful ones to come forth of their galleys,
Come out murdered, chief renouncer of Baptism,
Then through ambush they will pay him his wages.

80
The duke will want to exterminate his followers,
He will send the strongest ones to strange places:
Through tyranny to ruin Pisa and Lucca,
Then the Barbarians will gather the grapes without vine.

81
The crafty king will understand his snares,
Enemies to assail from three sides:
A strange number tears from hoods,
The grandeur of the translator will come to fail.

82
The great city having been long Besieged,
By an Innundation and violent plague,
The Sentinal and watch being surprised,
Shall be taken on a sudden, but hurt by no body.

83
Sun twentieth of taurus the earth will tremble very mightily,
It will ruin the great theater filled:
To darken and trouble air, sky and land,
Then the infidel will call upon god and saints.

84

The king exposed will complete the slaughter,
After he hath found out his offspring,
A Torrent shall open the sepulcher, made of marble and lead,
Of a great Roman, with a Medusean ensign.

85

To pass Gascony, Languedoc and the Rhône,
From agen holding Marmande and La Réole:
To open through faith the wall, Marseilles will hold its throne,
Conflict near Saint-Paul-de-Mausole.

86

From Bourg-la-Reine they will come straight to Chartres,
And near Pont d'Antony they will pause:
Seven crafty as Martens for peace,
Paris closed by an army they will enter.

87

By the forest Touphon cut off,
By the Hermitage shall the temple be set,
The duke of Estampes by his invented trick,
Shall give example to the prelate of Montlehery.

88

Calais, Arras, help to Thérouanne,
Peace and semblance the spy will simulate:
The soldiery of Savoy to descend by Roanne,
People who would end the rout deterred.

89

For seven years fortune will favor Philip,
He will beat down again the exertions of the Arabs:
Then at his noon perplexing contrary affair,
Young Ogmios will destroy his stronghold.

90

A captain of the great Germany,
Shall come to yield himself with a fained help,
Unto the king of kings, help of Hungary,
So that his revolt shall cause a great bloodshed.

91

The horrible plague Perinthus and Nicopolis,
The Peninsula and Macedonia will it fall upon:
It will devastate Thessaly and Amphipolis,
An unknown evil, and from Anthony refusal.

92

The king shall desire to enter into the new city,
With foes they shall come to overcome it,
The prisoner being free, shall speak and act falsly,
The king being gotten out, shall keep far from enemies.

93

The enemies being a good way from the fort,
The bastion brought by wagons:
Above the walls of Bourges crumbled,
When Hercules the Macedonian will strike.

94

Weak Galleys shall be united together,
False enemies, the strongest shall be fortified,
Weak ones assailed Bratislava trembles,
Lübeck and Meissen will take the barbarian side.

95

The newly made one will lead the army,
Almost cut off up to near the bank:
Help from the Milanais elite straining,
The duke deprived of his eyes in Milan in an iron cage.

96
The army denied entry to the city,
The duke will enter through persuasion:
The army led secretly to the weak gates,
Shall put all to fire and sword.

97
A fleet being divided into three parts,
The victuals will fail the second part,
Being in despaire they'l seek the Elysian fields,
And entring the breach first, shall obtain victory.

98
Those afflicted through the fault of a single one stained,
The transgressor in the opposite party:
He will send word to those of Lyons that compelled
They be to deliver the great chief of Molite.

99
The North wind shall cause the Siege to be raised,
They shall throw ashes, lime, and dust,
By a rain after that shall be a trap to them,
It shall be the last succours against their frontier.

100
Naval battle night will be overcome,
By fire, to the ships of the West ruine shall happen,
A new stratagem, the great ship coloured,
Anger to the vanquished, and victory in a mist.

CENTURY X

1

To the enemy, the enemy faith promised,
Shall not be kept, the prisoners shall be detained,
The first taken, put to death, and the rest stripped,
Giving the remnant that they may be succoured.

2

The galley and the ship shall hide their sails,
The great fleet shall make the little one to come out,
Ten ships near hand, shall turn and push at it,
The great being vanquished, they shall unite together.

3

After that, five shall not put out his flock,
He'l let loose a runnaway for Penelon,
There shall be a false rumour, succours shall come then,
The commander shall forsake the siege.

4

About midnight the leader of the army,
Shall save himself, vanishing suddenly,
Seven years after his fame shall not be blamed,
And at his return he shall never say yea.

5

Albi and Castres will form a new league,
Nine Arians Lisbon and the portuguese:
Carcassonne and Toulouse will end their intrigue,
When the chief new monster from the Lauraguais.

6

The Gardon will flood Nîmes so high
That they will believe Deucalion reborn:
Into the colossus the greater part will flee,
Vesta tomb fire to appear extinguished.

7

The great conflict that they are preparing for Nancy,
The Macedonian will say I subjugate all:
The British isle in anxiety over wine and salt,
"Hem. mi." Philip two Metz will not hold for long.

8

With forefinger and thumb he will moisten the forehead,
The Count of Senigallia to his own son:
The Venus through several of thin forehead,
Three in seven days wounded dead.

9
In the castle of Figueras on a misty day
From an infamous woman shall be born a sovereign prince,
His surname shall be from breeches, himself a posthume,
Never a king was worse in his province.

10
Endeavour of murder, enormous adulteries,
A great enemy of all mankind,
That shall be worse then grand-father, uncle, or father,
In iron, fire, water, bloody and inhumane.

11
At the dangerous passage below Junquera,
The posthumous one will have his band cross:
To pass the Pyrenees mountains without his baggage,
From Perpignan the duke will hasten to Tende.

12
Elected for a pope, from elected shall be baffled,
Upon a sudden, moved quick and fearful,
By too much sweetness provooked to die,
His fear being out in the night shall be leader to his death.

13
Beneath the food of ruminating animals,
led by them to the belly of the fodder city:
Soldiers hidden, their arms making a noise,
Tried not far from the city of Antibes.

14
Urnel Vaucile without a purpose on his own,
Bold, timid, through fear overcome and captured:
Accompanied by several pale whores,
Convinced in the Carthusian convent at Barcelona.

15
A father duke, aged and very thirsty,
In his extremity, his son denying him the ever,
Alive into a well, where he shall be drowned,
For which the senate shall give the son a long and easie death.

16
Happy in the kingdom of France, happy in his life,
Ignorant of blood, death, fury, of taking by force,
By no flatterers shall be envied,
King robbed, too much faith in kitchen.

17
The convict queen seeing her daughter pale,
Because of a sorrow locked up in her breast:
Lamentable cries will come then from Angoulême,
And the marriage of the first cousin impeded.

18

The house of Lorraine will make way for Vendôme,
The high put low, and the low put high:
The son of Mammon will be elected in Rome,
And the two great ones will be put at a loss.

19

The day that she shall be saluted queen,
The next day after the evening prayer,
All accompts being summoned and cast up,
She that was humble before, never was one so proud.

20

All the friends that shall have taken the part
Of the unlearned, put to death and robbed,
Goods sold publickly by proclamation, a great man seized of them,
Never Roman people was so much abused.

21

To spite the king, who took the part of the weaker,
He shall be murdered, presenting to him jewels,
The father and the son going to vex the nobility,
It shall be done to them as the magi did in Persia.

22

For not consenting to the divorce,
Which afterwards shall be acknowledged unworthy,
The king of the island shall be expelled by force,
And another subrogated, who shall have no mark of a king.

23

The remonstrances being made to the ungrateful people,
At that time the army shall seize upon Antibes,
In the river of Monaco they shall make their complaints,
And at Frejus both of them shall take their share.

24

The captive prince vanquished in Italy,
Shall pass by sea through Genoa to Marseilles,
By great endeavours of forrain forces overcome,
But that a barrel of honey shall save him from the fire.

25

Through the Ebro to open the passage of Bisanne,
Very far away will the Tagus make a demonstration:
In Pelligouxe will the outrage be committed,
By the great lady seated in the orchestra.

26

The successour shall avenge his bother in law,
Shall hold by force the kingdom, upon pretence of revenge,
That hinderance shall be killed, his dead blood ashamed,
A long time shall Brittany hold with France.

27

Charles the Fifth, and one great Hercules,
Shall open the temple with a warlike hand,
One Colonne, Julius and Ascan put back,
Spain, the key, eagle were never at such variance.

28

Second and third that make prime music,
Shall by the king be exalted to honour,
By a fat one, and a lean one, one in consumption,
A false report of Venus shall pull her down.

29

In a cave of Saint-Paul-de-Mausole a goat
Hidden and seized pulled out by the beard:
Led captive like a mastiff beast
By the Bigorre people brought to near Tarbes.

30

Nephew and blood of the saint newly come,
By the surname upholdeth vaults and covering,
They shall be driven, put to death, and driven out naked.
They shall change their red and black into green.

31

The holy empire shall come into Germany,
The Ismaelites shall find open places,
Asses shall also come out of Caramania,
Taking their part, and covering the earth.

32

The great empire, every one would be of it,
One above the rest shall obtain it,
But his time and his reign shall last little,
He may maintain himself two years in his shipping.

33
The cruel faction in the long robe
Will come to hide under the sharp daggers:
The duke to seize Florence and the diphthong place,
Its discovery by immature ones and sycophants.

34
The Gaul who will hold the empire through war,
He will be betrayed by his minor bother-in-law:
He will be drawn by a fierce, prancing horse,
The bother will be hated for the deed for a long time

35
The younger son of the king flagrant in burning lust
To enjoy his first cousin:
Female attire in the temple of Artemis,
Going to be murdered by the unknown one of Maine.

36
Upon the king of the stump speaking of wars,
The united isle will hold him in contempt:
Some good years gnawing one and plundering,
And by tyranny shall change the price of the island.

37
The great assembly near the lake of Bourget,
They will meet near Montmélian:
Going beyond the thoughtful ones will draw up a plan,
Chambéry, Saint-Jean-de-Maurienne, Saint-Julien combat.

38
Sprightly love lays the siege not far,
The garrisons will be at the barbarian saint:
The Orsini and Adria will provide a guarantee for the Gauls,
For fear delivered by the army to the Grisons.

39

Of the first son a widow, an unhappy match,
Without any children, two islands at variance,
Before eighteen an incompetant age,
Of the other lower shall be the agreement.

40

The young heir to the British realm,
Whom his father dying shall have recommended,
After his death London shall give him a topick,
And shall ask the kingdom from his son.

41

On the boundary of Caussade and Caylus,
Not at all far from the bottom of the valley:
Music from Villefranche to the sound of lutes,
Encompassed by cymbals and great stringing.

42

The humane reign of an angelical brood,
Shall cause his reign to be in peace and union,
Shall make war, captive shutting it half up,
He shall cause them to keep peace a great while.

43

The time too good, too much of royal bounty,
Made and unmade, nimble, quick, negligence,
Fickle shall believe false o' his loyal spouse,
He shall be put to death for his good will.

44

When a king will be against his people,
A native of Blois will subjugate the Ligurians,
Memel, Cordoba and the Dalmatians,
Of the seven then the shadow to the king, New Year's money and ghosts.

45

The shadow of the reign of Navarre not true,
Shall make the life of illegitimate chance,
The uncertain allowance from Cambray,
King of Orleans shall give a lawfull wall.

46

In life, fate and death a sordid, unworthy man of gold,
He will not be a new elector of Saxony:
From Brunswick he will send for a sign of love,
The false seducer delivering it to the people.

47

At the Garland lady of the town of Burgos,
They will impose for the treason committed:
The great prelate of leon through Formande,
Undone by false pilgrims and ravishers.

48

From the utmost part of old Spain,
Going out of the extremities of Europe,
He that troubled the travellers by the bridge of Laigne,
Shall have his great troop defeated by another.

49

Garden of the world, near the new city,
In the way of the digged mountains,
Shall be seized on, and thrown into the Tub,
Being forced to drink sulphurous poisoned waters.

50

The Meuse by day in the land of Luxembourg,
It will find Saturn and three in the urn:
Mountain and plain, town, city and borough,
Flood in Lorraine, betrayed by the great urn.

51

Some of the lowest places of the land of Lorraine
Will be united with the low Germans:
Through those of the see Picards, Normans, those of Main,
And they will be joined to the cantons.

52

At the place where the Lys and the Scheldt unite,
Shall the nuptials be, that were long a doing.
In the place of Antwerp where they draw the grape,
The young unspotted will comfort the old age.

53

The three concubines shall fight one with another a far off,
The greatest less shall remain watching,
The great Selin shall be no more their patron,
And shall call it fire, pelte, white, route.

54
She born in this world of a furtive concubine,
At two raised high by the sad news:
She will be taken captive by her enemies,
And brought to Malines and Brussels.

55
The unfortunate nuptials will be celebrated
In great joy but the end unhappy:
Husband and mother will slight the daughter-in-law,
The Apollo dead and the daughter-in-law more pitiful.

56
Royal prelate bowing himself too much,
A great flood of Blood shall come out of his mouth,
The English reign by reign respited,
A great while dead, alive in Tunis like a log.

57
The exalted shall not know his scepter
He shall put to shame the young children of the greatest,
Never was one more dirty and cruel,
He shall banish to black death their spouses.

58
In the time of mourning the feline monarch
Will make war upon the young Macedonian:
Gaul to shake, the bark to be in jeopardy,
Marseilles to be tried in the West a talk.

59
Within Lyons twenty-five of one mind,
Five citizens, Germans, Bressans, Latins:
Under a noble one they will lead a long train,
And discovered by barks of mastiffs.

60

I weep for Nice, Monaco, Pisa, Genoa,
Savona, Siena, Capua, Modena, Malta:
For the above blood and sword for a New Year's gift,
Fire, the earth will tremble, water an unhappy reluctance.

61

Betta, Vienna, Emorte, Sopron,
They will want to deliver Pannonia to the Barbarians:
Enormous violence through pike and fire,
The conspirators discovered by a matron.

62

Near Sorbin, to invade Hungary,
The herald of Buda shall come to give them notice of it,
Byzantine chief, Salona of Slavonia,
He will come to convert them to the law of the Arabs.

63

Cydonia, Ragusa, the city of St. Jerome,
With healing help to grow green again:
The king's son dead because of the death of two heroes,
Araby and Hungary will take the same course.

64

Weep Milan, weep Lucca and Florence,
When the great duke shall go upon the chariot,
To change the siege near Venice he goeth about,
When colonne shall change at Rome.

65

O great Rome thy ruine draweth near,
Not of thy walls, of thy blood and substance,
The sharp by letters shall make so horrid a notch,
Sharp iron thrust in all to the haft.

66

The chief of London by reign of America,
The island of Scotland shall catch thee by a frost,
King and Reb shall have so false an aAntichrist,
As will put them altogether by the ears.

67

The earthquake shall be so great in the month of May,
Saturn in capricorn, Jupiter and Mercury in taurus:
Venus also, cancer, Mars in virgo,
Hail will fall larger than an egg.

68

The fleet shall stand before the city,
Then shall go away for a little while,
And then shall take a great troop of citizens on land,
Fleet shall come back and recover a great deal.

69

The bright actions of new old exalted,
Shall be so great through the south and north,
By his own sister great forces shall be raised,
Running away he shall be murdered near the bush of Ambellon.

70

Through an object the eye will swell very much,
Burning so much that the snow will fall:
The fields watered will come to shrink,
As the primate succumbs at Reggio.

71

The earth and the air shall freeze with so much water,
When they shall come to worship Thursday,
That which shall be never, was so fair,
From the four parts they shall come to honour him.

72

In the year a thousand nine hundred ninety nine, and seven months,
From heaven a great terrible king,
To bring back to life the great king of the Mongols,
Before and after Mars to reign by good luck.

73

The present time together with the past
Will be judged by the great Joker:
The world too late will be tired of him,
And through the clergy oath-taker disloyal.

74

The year of the great seventh number accomplished,
It will appear at the time of the games of slaughter:
Not far from the great millennial age,
When the buried will go out from their tombs.

75

So long expected shall never come
Into Europe, in Asia shall appear,
One come forth of the line of the great Hermes,
And shall grow above all the kings in the east.

76

The great Senate will ordain the triumph
To one who after shall be vanquished and expelled,
The goods of his partners shall be
Publicly sold, and the enemy shall be driven away.

77

Thirty adherents of the order of Quirites
Banished, their possessions given their adversaries:
All their benefits will be taken as misdeeds,
Fleet dispersed, delivered to the corsairs.

78

Sudden joy shall turn into a sudden sadness,
At Rome to the embraced graces,
Mourning, cries, weeping, tears, blood, excellent joy,
Contrary troops surprized and carryed away.

79

The old roads will all be improved,
One will proceed on them to the modern Memphis:
The great Mercury of Hercules fleur-de-lis,
Causing to tremble lands, sea and country.

80

In the great reign, of the great reign reigning,
By force of arms the great brass gates,
He shall cause to be open, the king being joyned with the duke,
Haven demolish'd, ship sunk on a fair day.

81

A treasure put in a temple by Hesperian citizens,
In the same hid in a secret place,
The hungry bonds shall cause the temple to be open,
And take again and ravish, a fearful prey in the middle

82

Cries, weeping, tears, shall come with daggers,
With a false seeming they shall give the last assault,
Set round about they shall plant deep,
Beaten back alive, and murdered upon a sudden.

83

The signal to give battle will not be given,
They will be obliged to go out of the park:
The banner around Ghent will be recognized,
Of him who will cause all his followers to be put to death.

84
The illegitimate girl so high, high, not low,
The late return will make the grieved ones contended:
The reconciled one will not be without debates,
In employing and losing all his time.

85
The old tribune on the point of trembling,
Shall be much intreated not to deliver the captain,
They will not will, the ill speaking fearful,
By legitimate shall deliver to his friends.

86
As a griffin shall come the king of Europe,
Accompanied with those of the north,
Of red and white shall conduct a great troop,
And they shall go against the king of Babylon.

87
A great king shall land by Nice,
The great empire of death shall interpose with it.
In Antibes will he place his heifer,
The plunder by sea all will vanish.

88
Foot and horse upon the second watch,
Shall come in destroying all by sea,
They shall come into the harbour of Marseilles,
Tears, cryes and blood, never was so bitter a time.

89
The walls shall be turned from brick into marble,
There shall be peace for seven and fifty years,
Joy to mankind, the aqueduct shall be built again,
Health, abundance of fruit, joy and mellifluous time.

90

The inhumane tyrant shall die a hundred times,
In his place shall be put a learned and mild man,
All the senate shall be at his command,
He shall be made angry by a rash malicious person.

91

The Roman clergy in the year a thousand six hundred and nine,
In the beginning of the year shall make choice
Of a gray and black, come out of the country,
Such a one as never a worse was.

92

The child shall be killed before the fathers eyes,
The father after shall enter into ropes of rushes,
The people of Geneva shall notably stir themselves,
The chief lying in the middle like a log.

93

The new bark will take trips,
There and near by they will transfer the empire:
Beaucaire, Arles will retain the hostages,
Near by, two columns of Porphyry found.

94

Scorn from Nîmes, from Arles and Vienne,
Not to obey the Hesperian edict:
To the tormented to condemn the great one,
Six escaped in seraphic garb.

95

A most potent king shall come into Spain,
Who by sea and land shall make great conquests towards the south,
This evil shall beat down the horns of the new moon,
And slack the wings of those of Friday.

96

The Religion of the name of the seas will win out
Against the sect of the son of Adaluncatif:
Obstinate sect deplorate shall be afraid,
Of the two wounded by Aleph and Aleph.

97

Triremes full of captives of all age.
Time good for evil, the sweet for bitter,
Pray to the barbarian, they shall be too hasty,
Desirous to see the feather complain in the wind.

98

The clear splendour of the merry maid,
Shall shine no more, she shall be a great while without salt,
With merchants, ruffans, wolves, odious,
All promiscuously, she shall be an universal monster.

99

The end of wolf, lion, ox and ass,
Timid deer they will be with mastiffs:
No longer will the sweet manna fall upon them,
More vigilance and watch for the mastiffs.

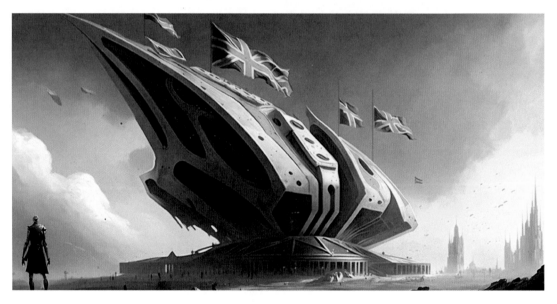

100

The great empire shall be in England,
The all-powerful for more then three hundred years,
Great armies shall pass through sea and land,
The Lusitanians shall not be contented therewith.